CHICAGO'S | *Greatest Sports Memories*

Edited by
Roland Lazenby

Sports Publishing Inc.
www.SportsPublishingInc.com

Chicago Sun-Times

Chicago's Greatest Sports Memories

Edited by Roland Lazenby

Joanna L. Wright, Coordinating Editor

Bill Adee, *Chicago Sun-Times* Executive Sports Editor
Nancy Stuenkel, *Chicago Sun-Times* Photo Editor
Joseph J. Bannon, Jr., Supervising Editor
Terrence Miltner, Research Editor
Erin J. Sands, Production Coordinator, Book Design
Jeff Higgerson, Dustjacket Design
David Hamburg, Copy Editor

ISBN: 1-58382-060-4

Published by Sports Publishing Inc.
www.SportsPublishingInc.com

ACKNOWLEDGMENTS

hicago has been home to some of sports' most historic moments. Most of them have been great; some of them were not so great. But all of them have been memorable.

The century began with the Sox (1906) and Cubs (1907-08) combining to win three World Series titles and closed with the Bulls' six NBA championships in the 1990s. In between, Chicago fans witnessed the Black Sox scandal; the emergence of pro football under the Bears' George Halas and Red Grange; the boxing championships of Jack Dempsey, Joe Louis and Sugar Ray Robinson; baseball's first All-Star Game at Comiskey; Ruth's "called" shot; George Mikan's dominance of college basketball; Ernie Banks' greatness; Blackhawk championships; high school heroes; the unmatched efforts of Gale Sayers and Dick Butkus; the collapse of the '69 Cubs; Ray Meyer's victory ride to the Final Four; Notre Dame football; the brilliance of Walter Payton; the sheer joy of "The Super Bowl Shuffle"; lights at Wrigley; a Northwestern Rose Bowl appearance; and the power of Sammy Sosa.

For all these memorable moments—and for many more—the *Chicago Sun-Times* and its predecessor papers have given Chicago fans a front-row seat for each historic event. Bringing these moments to life every day in the paper takes the hard work and dedication of many people. In putting this book together, we received the overwhelming support of the entire *Sun-Times* staff. In particular, we would like to acknowledge the efforts of executive sports editor Bill Adee, photo editor Nancy Stuenkel and librarian Terri Golembiewski.

Space limitations preclude us from thanking each writer whose work appears in this book. However, whenever available, we have preserved the writers' bylines to ensure proper attribution for their work. Likewise, it is not possible to thank each photographer whose work appears herein. Nevertheless, we would be remiss not to acknowledge the photo contributions of Richard A. Chapman, Tom Cruze, Robert A. Davis, Rich Hein, Brian Jackson, Dom Najolia, Jon Sall, and Phil Velasquez.

And finally, I am grateful for all the support and hard work of those at Sports Publishing Inc. who assisted me on this project: Joe Bannon Jr., Erin Sands, Susan McKinney, David Hamburg, Jeff Higgerson, Terrence Miltner, and Terry Hayden.

Joanna L. Wright
Coordinating Editor

CONTENTS

INTRODUCTION

by Roland Lazenby

Sometimes the past and the future come face-to-face. I remember thinking that as I stood inside the brand-new United Center one night in early March 1994 and watched a high-tech introduction to "Your World-Champion Chicago Bulls."

Then I walked outside, just north across Madison Street, to visit the past—the remains of Chicago Stadium. In the dusk of that Wednesday, the Stadium stood as silent and eerie as a graveyard. During the ensuing months, demolition crews would persistently digest the grand, old "sandstone sarcophagus," eating away first at the insides, then attacking the shell, until only the steel framework and neat piles of rubble remained.

That night, the old building stood with a gigantic hole knocked in its west wall, revealing an interior still largely intact. For the ticket holders arriving for that night's game, it was unsettling to see the giant wound in this landmark. Even stranger, the lights were on inside, as if the spirits of games past were anxiously awaiting the crowd's arrival for another tipoff.

Just months earlier, the two buildings' circumstances had been reversed. At that time, the United Center was a framework under construction, standing silently, while the Stadium, the "Madhouse on Madison," thundered with the exhortations of some 18,676 fans. On this night, though, the only sound in the Stadium was the relentless Chicago wind pushing through the vast hole and rattling the lights. Soon the Stadium would fade altogether, into a parking lot.

From time to time during his workday, Tim Hallam, the Bulls' director of media services, retreated from his

Charles Comiskey (left) and William Wrigley Jr.

Globetrotters founder Abe Saperstein and Wilt Chamberlain

building just drove the noise down right over the floor, and it just hovered there. It made it impossible to hear anything."

Everyone, it seems, has a favorite recollection of this impossibility. When was it the loudest? For many, that date is May 1989, Game 6 of the Eastern Conference finals, the Bulls versus the Detroit Pistons. Toward the end of the third quarter, Pistons center Bill Laimbeer, that dastardly villain, stepped to the free throw line, and somehow the same thought was instantly and magically transmitted into the minds of the 18,676 people in attendance.

"Laim-beer sucks! Laim-beer sucks! Laim-beer sucks!" they intoned over and over until, sadly, he canned both shots.

Kip Motta, son of former Bulls coach Dick Motta, likes to think of the 1974 playoffs, when he was a young ball boy and the Bulls were facing the Pistons at home for Game 7 of their playoff battle. Jerry Sloan, the team's gutty leader, had been injured in Game 6 in Detroit and was unable to play. "We were warming up," Motta recalled, "and you could tell there was no excitement. It was like a cloud of doom over us because Jerry wasn't

spacious office in the United Center to the sidewalk outside for a smoke. These retreats were a bit uncomfortable because Hallam, who had worked games at the Stadium for 17 years, didn't like looking at the grand, old building in its hour of demise. He couldn't quite bring himself to gather with the crowd that witnessed the wrecking ball first striking the west wall. "It was a little bit of a funeral," he explained.

Even Bulls chairman Jerry Reinsdorf, the man who built the United Center with the help of Blackhawks chairman Bill Wirtz, admitted to feeling unsettled by the sight of the Stadium going down. "But it's just a building," he said. "It needed to be replaced. What's important are the memories of what happened there, and the memories will live for a long time."

Research suggests that the senses drive the memory, so the Stadium is destined—like her sister building, Boston Garden—to be remembered for the peculiar smells of old arenas, decades of stale popcorn and spilled beer and sweat.

As pungent as these odors were, the overriding sensory impact of the Stadium was the noise itself. "There was no place like Chicago Stadium," said former Bulls general manager Rod Thorn. "The acoustics in that old

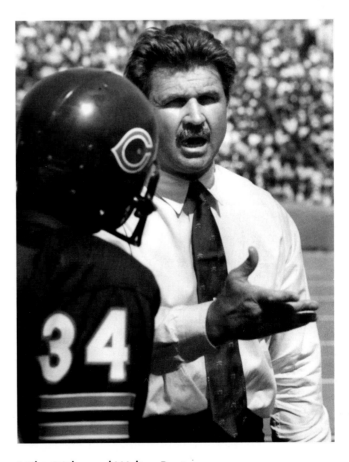

Mike Ditka and Walter Payton

7

Demolition at Old Comiskey Park

gonna play. But when he came up out of the locker room on his crutches, the crowd gave him a standing ovation. It was the loudest, most intense ovation I've ever heard. It was unbelievable. They went crazy. For four or five minutes, they didn't stop. And it got louder and louder all the time."

Buoyed by the fan support, the Bulls pulled together and beat Detroit to win the series.

"I was reluctant to even go up there," Sloan remembered. "But I wanted to watch the game."

Later, he served as the longtime coach of the Utah Jazz, but Sloan's fondest Chicago memories are of the Stadium. "I spent a great deal of my life in basketball in that building," he said, "and it was one of the greatest places if you were a player. . . . These days people talk about noisy buildings, but a lot of that is electronic, manufactured noise. There wasn't much going on back in the Stadium except people yelling and raising hell every time they came out to the game. If they came, they came to yell. They didn't come to see who was

gonna look at them and see what they looked like. There weren't very many people sitting there in mink coats, either. It was hard-core fans.

"And they'd boo your ass, too, if you didn't play well," Sloan recalled with a grin. "We were getting beat one night against New York. The Knicks had us down 28 points at halftime, and our fans booed us off the floor. We responded to it. We came right back out in the second half and beat the Knicks, and that's when New York was good, when they had Willis Reed and Walt Frazier and that bunch."

"The loudest I ever heard it," said Hallam, "was when Jerry Sloan was coaching and we were playing the Knicks in the best-of-three miniseries in the first round of the 1981 playoffs and we went to overtime.

"That was back when people were smoking in the upper balconies and you had the haze hanging over the floor. That's why it was such a great—I don't want to say it—but a great 'sixth man.' It was so loud, it was crazy. You weren't exactly fearful, but you could tell that anything could happen. It was very intimidating for officials, for visiting teams, because it looked like all hell could break loose at any time."

Standing there at dusk in 1994, I could almost hear the echoes of these and a thousand other events—Blackhawks Stanley Cup victories, prizefights, ice shows, Globetrotter comedy hours, even an NFL game or two, including the Bears' 1932 victory over Providence, which decided the NFL championship that year.

This book intends to keep alive the grand moments of the Stadium, old Comiskey Park and the city's other sports venues, all with their attendant special memories. Some of the stories here happened well outside the city's limits, but the events still rang through Chicago's canyons, causing minds to race and hearts to flutter.

For old-time's sake, we've attempted to repeat that trick here, with samplings from the *Sun-Times* and the old *Daily News.*

Like the Stadium and the United Center, it's a mix of the old and the new, the happy and the sad, with plenty of the broad-shoulders stuff that makes Chicago the greatest of sports towns.

Michael Jordan's 1993 retirement press conference

It had grown rather quickly from a collection of prairie mud huts and outhouses in the early 19th century, so that by 1900, Chicago was in full industrial bloom, a town of mail order and slaughter and steel and retail and banking and a hundred other things that throbbed up in the iron ring of its Loop. It had been rebuilt after the fire of 1871, until it stood on the brink of a new century as a technological wonder, its electric streetlights and skyscrapers and noisy, sparkling streetcars creating a sense of awe in visitors.

Novelist Frank Norris proclaimed that Chicago "throbbed the true life—the true power and spirit of America."

Between the cracks, there was also the obvious grime, enough prostitution and graft and mayhem to color the city's image for decades to come.

Altogether, it was the kind of place where people kept score, where they took the big view when it came to amusing themselves, where competition found a natural, healthy appetite.

In April of 1900, Charles A. Comiskey brought his St. Paul Saints to town, renamed them the White Sox and set up shop in the little wooden confines at 39th and Wentworth. Comiskey, the son of an alderman, aimed to compete with the crosstown National Leaguers.

By the next season, the National League team had such a young cast that two sportswriters—George Rice and Fred Hayner—nicknamed them the Cubs and even drew up a little logo to illustrate it. It would be six more seasons before the team would officially adopt the nickname, but fans quickly embraced the concept and became "Cub backers."

When the two teams met in the "world's series" in 1906, the city seemingly set all other matters aside to focus on the outcome. It was a "streetcar" series, the inhabitants of the city's neighborhoods crisscrossing town to follow the "White Stockings'" victory, four games to two.

Downcast in the aftermath, Cub backers would find reason to celebrate in 1907 as Joe Tinker, Johnny Evers and Frank Chance led Chicago's National Leaguers to a 4-2 victory over Detroit in the World Series. Then the very next year, they did it all over again, whipping the New York Giants in a National League playoff game, then jumping Ty Cobb and the Tigers again in five quick contests.

The site of this glory was a West Side playing field, near the current location of Cook County Hospital. In the old days, a mental sanitarium sat near left field, with many of its residents hanging out the windows to follow the innings. Chicago legend has it that the circumstances prompted the saying, "You're out in left field."

Cub backers certainly need no reminder that the 1908 Series provided their last taste of championship victory. The decade, however, provided plenty more for Chicago's nascent fan base to appreciate. Amos Alonzo Stagg directed his University of Chicago football team to the first of six championship seasons.

Little known is the fact that Stagg also participated in the original basketball game with Dr. James Naismith at the School for Christian Workers in Springfield, Massachusetts, in 1891. Stagg, like many other of those participants, would play a key role in the development of college hoops in Chicago.

The big story in the first decade of the century, however, was baseball, and those first three championships sealed the deal on what would become the city's long-running love affair with the diamond's sweet science.

Nothing symbolized Chicago sports at the turn of the century more than the Cubs' famed trio of shortstop Joe Tinker, second baseman Johnny Evers and first baseman Frank Chance. The three starters were immortalized in a poem written by sportswriter Franklin P. Adams.

Quiet Settles on World Series Fans

Quiet reigns in the baseball camps and already the players on the Chicago National League Cub team are preparing to make their "get away" to the far corners. They only wish to live down the loss and never did a bunch of favorites feel worse than these same Cubs, though, as Capt. Chance expressed it at a little gathering last night, he "did not mind losing to Comiskey."

Generally speaking, Chicago fans one and all expressed themselves as glad the agony was over. Never had there been so much excitement in this town of a continuous nature which involved all classes as did the recent clash of Cubs and Sox.

"My clerks can now get their minds back on business," said one manager ruefully, and even he admitted that he had been up in the air with the rest of the bunch. Orders had piled up on him and clerks were absent and the town was seized with the "bug" such as never had occurred before.

"The day after" for the winners and losers in the great world's series, which ended yesterday on the south side grounds, was a comparatively quiet one. The fans who have been worked up to such a high state of excitement during the past week all settled back today into the regular routine of the business life and in a few days Chicago will have fully recovered from the frenzied state of delirium that it has been in for the past three days. There were many more White Stocking rooters to be seen today than Cub backers. Only the most ardent of the west side rooters would admit that they ever had pulled for the Cubs to win and many of those that were weak-kneed pointed at by some of their glorying friends.

"It would take something like an invading army to command so much real respect," said one man, "as was accorded to the baseball men. Many west siders and north siders will take some time to settle down and find excuses for altering their opinions. Never were favorites so jarred as were the Cubs and up here on the north side we figure that the hard fight the Sox made to win their own pennant gave them the strength to go on and show the Cubs up. The Cubs certainly fell off in their game and could not get going again, and that's the way it looks to me."

—————— "There is one thing I will never believe, and that is the White Sox are a better ball club than the Cubs. We did not play our game, and that's all there is to it."

—Cubs player/manager Frank Chance

Known as the "Hitless Wonders," the 1906 world champion White Sox batted a miserly .230 (worst in the AL), with only seven home runs for the entire season. Reported the local media: "To those who have not seen the Sox in their wonderful [19-game] winning streak, it is a wonder how they score so many runs on so few hits. Let them see the Sox take every advantage of misplays and let them see them dash daringly around the bases and invite wild throws . . . . These wonderful fans will then solve for themselves the methods which are winning game after game." Winners of 93 games during the season, the White Sox defeated the Chicago Cubs, 4-2, in the city's only crosstown World Series.

Cubs Retain Honors

Manager Frank Chance and his Cubs are twice winners of the world's baseball championship. It is the first time in the history of baseball that a team has won the highest honors in the game twice.

By winning the fifth game of the world's series from the Detroit Tigers yesterday by a 2-to-0 score, the Chicago National League team has established a record that is expected to stand for years to come. The Detroit men have won only one game out of the ten played in last year's and this year's world's championship series, showing they were outclassed.

The victory for the Cubs finished up the series, as it made four out of the five games for them. If the Tigers had won, the struggle would have been continued here this afternoon. The season of 1908 is now closed and the players will go into retirement until training time next spring.

The Cubs lost no time in winning the game. They made one run in the first inning, which proved enough to win for them. Their second tally was registered in the fifth round. Johnny Evers was the man who brought home the run in the first inning and Johnny Kling brought home the last run.

Three hits were made off Will Bill Donovan in the first inning that scored the one run for Chicago. Jimmy Sheckard was out when Evers pushed a single into center and Frank "Wildfire" Schulte followed with another single, which put Evers on second. Chance then came up and smashed a hit into center, which brought Evers home. Solly Hofman hit to Bill Coughlin and forced Schulte on the line after Harry Steinfeldt had gone out on a fly to Sam Crawford.

The Cubs made their second run in the fifth. Charley O'Leary made a great play on Joe Tinker's fly and held it, but Kling got his base on balls. Orval Overall sacrificed and then Sheckard got another pass out of Donovan. Evers smashed the first ball pitched to him for two bases and scored Kling and put Sheckard on third, where he died, as Schulte went out by way of O'Leary.

A triumphant tour of the west, up and down the Pacific coast, is being arranged for Chicago's Cubs, two-time champions of the world. A guaranty of $10,000 has been posted by the San Francisco and Los Angeles clubs to get Chance and his world beaters out there and the owners of those two teams are anxious to put up a side wager of $15,000 that the coast teams will win a majority of the games played with the Cubs.

Fourteen players will go, if the trip is decided upon. Twelve have promised positively to go, one is undecided and the fourteenth has not yet been selected. Those who will go are Chance, Evers, Tinker, Steinfeldt, Schulte, Hofman, Sheckard, Del Howard, Kling, Pat Moran, Overall and Mordecai "Three Finger" Brown. Ed Reulbach probably will go also, making the third pitcher.

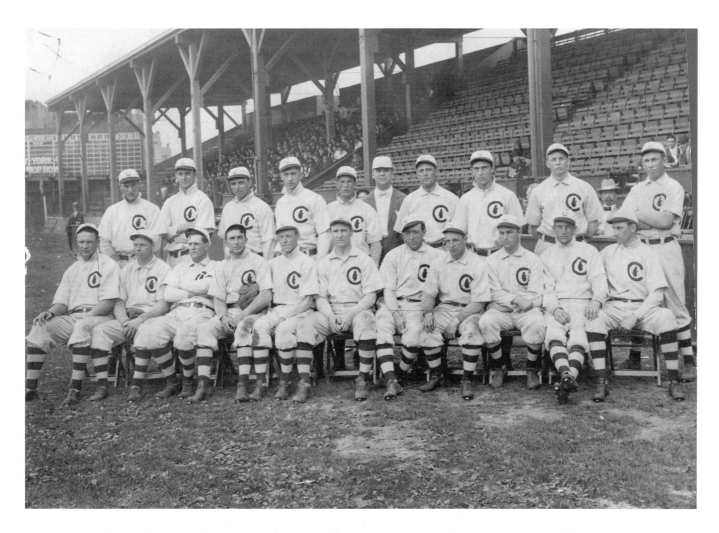

Most of the players in this 1907 Cubs team photo won a second consecutive World Series championship in 1908. Little did anyone know that the new century would arrive before another Cubs World Series title.

The Great Lakes cruise ship *Eastland* tipped over in the Chicago River on July 24, 1915, and 844 people, most of them Western Electric employees and their guests on a company outing, lost their lives.

This was clearly a decade of disaster for Chicago, as a succession of developments—meatpacking scandals, labor strife, world war, racial tension that erupted in a riot costing 38 lives and hundreds more injured and the growing influence of organized crime—all marked the city. It fell to sports to provide relief from these negative forces. And for a time, the competition did just that, with a fascinating flow of events. Fancy new Comiskey Park opened in July 1910, and the Sox marked the event with a loss to the St. Louis Browns. The new facility was so quickly overrun by gamblers that within months, 15 cops would be arrested at the park and charged with taking bribes from bookies. That fall of 1910 the Cubs played their way back into the World Series, only to fall short, four games to one, to the Philadelphia Athletics. Just two months later, businessmen gathered at a State Street meeting to found the National League of Colored Baseball, a seven-team alliance.

In July of 1913 the city hosted the international scholastic track-and-field meet, with local Oak Park High winning the event.

In 1914, a third pro baseball team, the Chicago Federals, opened for business in the city and played games at Weeghman Field, located at Clark and Addison. A year later, the Federals folded, and the Cubs quickly moved into their digs, beating the Cincinnati Reds in the first game there in April 1916. With the city's—not to mention the world's—focus on the growing conflict in Europe, the White Sox quietly thrashed the New York Giants, four games to two, to win the 1917 World Series. The war brought a shortening of the baseball season in 1918, but the Cubs still managed to claim the National League pennant, only to find themselves gulping in the face of Babe Ruth's pitching in the World Series. The Babe won two games for Boston, just the margin the Red Sox needed to triumph, four games to two. Likewise, the college football season was interrupted, so much so that the Great Lakes Navy team claimed the Rose Bowl that January of 1919.

Chicagoans were treated to yet another World Series that fall, as a star-laden White Sox club stepped up as heavy favorites over Cincinnati's Reds. The powerful but underpaid Sox began stumbling through inning after sorry inning, arousing Comiskey's suspicions that his players were doing business on the side. The ensuing scandal would ring through baseball for decades after it was revealed that eight players took money from gamblers to throw the Series. Soon dubbed the Black Sox, the eight were indicted for conspiracy to commit fraud. They won acquittal in the court case but lost their baseball careers to suspension.

Outside the courthouse after hearings on the matter opened, White Sox legend Shoeless Joe Jackson was confronted by a newsboy. "Say it ain't so, Joe," the 10-year-old supposedly pleaded, to which Jackson reportedly answered, "It's so, kid."

The century's second decade began with the opening of the White Sox's new ballpark.

The
American League Base Ball Club
of
Chicago

requests the honor of your presence
at the
Opening of White Sox Park
Friday afternoon, July the first
nineteen hundred and ten
at three o'clock

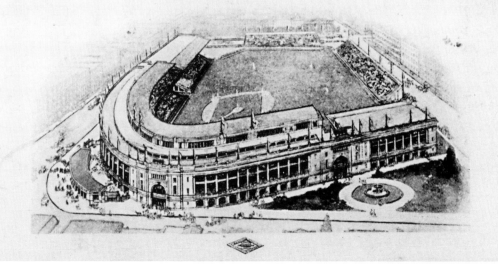

Vaughn and Toney Not Hit in 9 Innings

By Oscar C. Reichow

ub fans today saw one of the most remarkable pitching duels they probably ever have seen when Jim Vaughn and Fred Toney set a new world's baseball record by twirling no-hit ball for nine innings in the first game between the Cubs and Reds.

The final score: Cincinnati, 1; Cubs, 0.

First inning—Cincinnati: Heinie Groh struck out. Larry Kopf hit a roller to Larry Doyle and was thrown out. Greasy Neale hit the first ball, which Cy Williams caught. Cubs: Rollie Zeider crashed into the first ball, which Manuel Cueto got close to the foul line. Dave Shean ran to short center for Harry Wolter's fly. Doyle hit to Kopf and was thrown out.

Second inning—Cincinnati: Hal Chase popped a high bounder to Vaughn and was thrown out. Jim Thorpe hit to Doyle and was thrown out. Shean's pop fly was taken by Charlie Deal. Cubs: Fred Merkle went out on a line drive to Groh. Four balls put Williams on first. Groh came in on Les Mann's slow grounder and threw him out. Williams took second. Kopf got Art Wilson's high fly.

Third inning—Cincinnati: Doyle got Cueto's fly. Emil Huhn rolled to Vaughn and was tossed out. Toney struck out. Cubs: Deal hit sharply to Groh and was thrown out. Vaughn hit a roller to Chase and was out. Zeider popped to Chase.

Fourth inning—Cincinnati: Groh worked Vaughn for a pass. Kopf hit to Doyle, who chased Groh back toward first, then threw to Merkle, retiring Kopf. Merkle whipped the ball to Zeider, who doubled Groh. Neale reached first on Zeider's fumble. Neale was caught stealing. Cubs: Shean got under Wolter's high fly. Cueto got Doyle's fly. Merkle flied to Groh.

Fifth inning—Cincinnati: Chase struck out. A slow ball on the third strike retired Thorpe. Shean struck out. Cubs: Williams worked Toney for four balls. Mann's long fly was caught by Cueto. Shean dropped Wilson's high fly in back of first and Williams was retired when he stuck to first base. Neale hauled in Deal's drive.

Sixth inning—Cincinnati: Cueto was called out on strikes. Huhn rolled to Merkle and was out. Toney hit in front of the plate, and before he could get started for first was tagged by Wilson. Cubs: Vaughn looked at the third strike. Groh and Chase retired Zeider. Wolter's grounder caromed off Toney's bare hand, but Kopf threw him out.

Seventh inning—Cincinnati: Groh objected to two strikes and was banished. Gus Getz replaced him and drew a base on balls. Kopf forced Getz, Vaughn to Doyle, and was doubled at first, Doyle to Merkle. Neale popped to Wilson. Cubs: Getz went to third in Groh's place. Doyle hit to Chase and was retired. Merkle's hard bounder was taken by Kopf and he was thrown out. Shean got Williams' fly.

Eighth inning—Cincinnati: Chase popped to Doyle. Thorpe was called out on strikes. Shean fanned. Cubs: Cueto got Mann's fly. Wilson was thrown out by Kopf. Deal flied to Thorpe.

Ninth inning—Cincinnati: Cueto lined to Deal. Huhn was called out on strikes. Toney struck out. Cubs: Vaughn fouled to Getz. Getz threw out Zeider. Wolter flied to Getz.

Tenth inning—Cincinnati: Getz flied to Wilson. Kopf got the first hit of the game when he singled to right. Neale lifted to Williams. Williams dropped Chase's line drive and Kopf raced to third. Chase stole second. Thorpe hit in front of the plate and Kopf scored when Vaughn raced in, fielded the ball and tossed to Wilson, who was not looking for the play and missed the ball. Chase attempted to score on the same play, but was retired by Wilson. Cubs: Doyle struck out. Cueto backed against the fence and got Merkle's fly. Williams fanned.

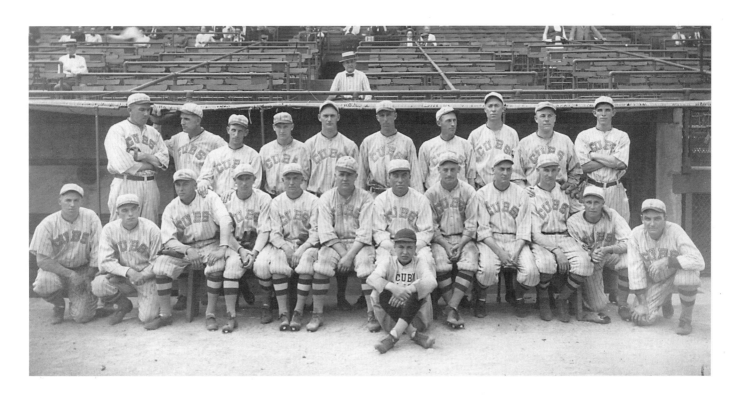

Cubs pitcher James "Hippo" Vaughn (standing, second from left) is considered by many to be the best left-handed pitcher in Cubs history. Vaughn is the Cubs' career leader for left-handers in wins (151), games started (270), complete games (177), shutouts (35), innings pitched (2,216.1) and strikeouts (1,138). During the Cubs' 1918 World Series season, Vaughn won pitching's triple crown—leading the National League in wins (22), strikeouts (148) and ERA (1.74). Vaughn's nine-inning no-hit duel with Reds pitcher Fred Toney in 1917 still stands as one of baseball's all-time greatest pitching performances.

Sox Win the World Championship

By George S. Robbins

"Champions of the World"—that's the title of the Chicago White Sox today and they deserve the laurels they have won from one of the strongest and most resourceful clubs ever assembled in the National League. Incidentally, Charles A. Comiskey, owner of the White Sox, is the happiest man in the whole world today.

It required able pitching, effective fielding, timely hitting and a classic boner to clinch the flag for Chicago. The score of 4 to 2 yesterday at the Polo Grounds before a crowd that about jammed the seating capacity of the park was a hard blow to the pride of Gotham.

Manager Clarence Rowland, the so-called busher leader, played his cards carefully and won a brilliant victory. Turning a deaf ear to the entreaties of his friends, the Sox leader sent Urban Faber, his pet pitcher and pride of Dubuque, to the firing line to end the series. Rowland's judgment was right. Faber was right, too. Gotham fans discovered this to their sorrow. Faber carried the heavy pitching burden of the series. He emerged the slab hero of the 1917 world's classic.

Faber pitched and won the second game of the series 7 to 2. He lost one contest in New York by the shutout route of 5 to 0. The Cascade and Dubuque product finished the fifth contest in Chicago won by the Sox 8 to 5. He was the pitching star of the final engagement, hurling the Sox to victory 4 to 2.

It is seldom that a pitcher has the honor of appearing in four games of a world's series. That Faber finished strong proves he is a real iron man of baseball.

Comiskey has reached the pinnacle of fame in sportdom. He can go no higher. When Heinie Zimmerman chased Comiskey's $50,000 infielder toward the home plate he was unconsciously making baseball history. He was inscribing his name in the book among the goats of all time in the world's series. He also was helping Comiskey and Rowland cinch a flag. He was helping round out the greatest career in the annals of sport. He was helping prove that the name of busher as applied to Rowland is a misnomer.

Winning a world's title means more to Comiskey at this time than it did in 1903. It is the biggest boost to baseball that could happen. It means the game will go on, despite all the dangers that are making the world a battle ground.

Comiskey has done more to help his country in this world war than any other sportsman. He has made his baseball plant a part of the machinery to aid the government. He has made his park a parade ground for Uncle Sam's soldiers and has contributed a part of his proceeds to aid in the Red Cross and other patriotic undertakings.

Comiskey will now probably take his team of world beaters around the globe, spreading the game in all countries. Not even the war can stop him. In fact, he will be aided by the government.

This world's title has "made" Clarence Rowland. This manager has "arrived" among the select set. He has made the fans like him despite the millstone of "busher" hung on him from the start.

Arnold "Chick" Gandil, who returned to the White Sox before the 1917 season, was one of the keys to their world championship that year.

If Chicago factored heavily in the besmirching of baseball, it also played a role in cleaning up the mess. Kenesaw Mountain Landis, the city's prominent federal judge, was named baseball commissioner in December of 1920 and would preside over the game for the next quarter century while posing as the fierce protector of its integrity.

Just three months earlier, the Black Sox scandal had wound its way to a grand jury indictment, prompting headlines in a city with a seemingly endless rush of big developments.

Regardless, the city's sports agenda rolled headlong into a new day. Notre Dame had stepped front and center, as college football found a burgeoning popularity as mass entertainment. Very quickly, the Big 10 schools and the Irish found themselves capable of drawing crowds of 100,000 on Saturday afternoons. Central in the growing legend for both Knute Rockne and Notre Dame was the sad fate of terminally ill star George Gipp, who made one of his final, brief appearances against Northwestern in Chicago in 1920.

The decade also brought the dawn of radio, first WMAQ, then WGN and, a few months later, WBBM in the Wrigley Building. It would take time for the ethics of amateur sports to accept the broadcasting of college games, but the groundwork had been laid for what would become the city's impressive array of sports media options.

In July of 1924, Johnny Weissmuller, a former altar boy in Chicago, sent Paris crowds into a frenzy by setting world freestyle records in the 100- and 400-meter events at the 1924 Olympics. His swimmer's physique would later serve him well, as he became the screen star of the Tarzan movies, which were adapted from the books of Edgar Rice Burroughs, another Windy City native.

That January of 1925, Rockne's Irish, sporting their heavily hyped Four Horsemen backfield, capped off a 9-0 season by dismissing Stanford 27-10 in the Rose Bowl.

It was a time when the press bestowed unparalleled nicknames upon college gridiron stars. The chief rival to the Four Horsemen of the Apocalypse was a three-time All-American for the University of Illinois dubbed the Galloping Ghost. Harold "Red" Grange displayed such a star quality that Bears coach George Halas shocked the sports world by signing Grange to a pro contract just days after his final appearance for the Illini. Halas then hustled Grange into a Bears uniform for a Thanksgiving Day game at Wrigley Field and later sent Grange and the Bears on an unprecedented postseason, nationwide barnstorming tour that drew tens of thousands of fans in every venue and brought millions into the empty coffers of pro football. Suddenly the National Football League, a struggling, backwater alliance, stepped into the center of a continuous media event. Everywhere Grange went, the newsreels and sportswriters followed.

Grant Park Field opened that same year (1925), and a few months later would be renamed Soldier Field. Cubs Park, meanwhile, gave up its old name to become Wrigley Field.

By then, Chicago was on its way to becoming quite a famous—and sometimes infamous—place, distinguished by Al Capone's violence, Jelly Roll Morton's blues, Carl Sandburg's poetry, Louis Armstrong's jazz and an unsurpassed corporate bounty, driven by a stock market that seemed like it would soar forever.

In the panorama, 1927 was marked by the legendary long count in the Dempsey-Tunney heavyweight fight before 105,000 fans at Soldier Field (estimated in the daily coverage reprinted here at 150,000). In a less noticed development, the year also brought the first organizational efforts of Chicagoan Abe Saperstein to form a traveling, all-black basketball team that would years hence come to be known as the Harlem Globetrotters.

By 1928, Weissmuller had capped a remarkable career (featuring 67 world records) with another gold in the 400-meter freestyle at the Amsterdam Olympics.

A year later, legendary manager Joe McCarthy directed a Cubs lineup featuring Rogers Hornsby, Gabby Hartnett and Hack Wilson to the World Series, where they had the misfortune to meet Jimmie Foxx and the Philadelphia Athletics, who promptly dominated, four games to one.

It was the same month, of course, that would bring the first dark quakes of economic collapse. The Chicago that had roared soon found itself strapped by soup lines and a sorrow that even the greatest moments, no matter how heavily hyped, could begin to address.

It was during the 1920s that pro football made its first mark on the sports map. At the forefront of this development was Chicago's George Halas, who founded the Decatur Staleys in 1920, moved them to Chicago in 1921 and renamed them the Bears in 1922.

Eight White Sox Indicted

Seven White Sox players and one former member of the team, including some of the most famous members of the American League team, were named in true bills following a reported statement by Eddie Cicotte involving all of them in a conspiracy to "throw" the world's series last fall.

Cicotte, it is learned, confessed that he received $10,000, and said that Joe Jackson asked for $20,000, but received only $5,000.

"I refused to pitch a ball until I got the money," Cicotte said. "It was placed under my pillow in the hotel the night before the first game of the Series. Everyone was paid individually, and the same scheme was used to deliver it."

Arnold "Chick" Gandil, former first baseman for the Sox, who is now playing outlaw ball in Idaho, Cicotte said, acted as the chief go-between in all the money deals. He is reported to have received $50,000 for his part in fixing the Series.

Jackson, in his statement to the jury, is reported to have told the same story Cicotte told.

Cicotte is said to have admitted that during the first game of the World Series last year he lost the game for the Sox by purposely intercepting a throw from the outfield which would have caught a Reds player at home and that later he made a wild throw which allowed another runner to score. This game was lost 2 to 1.

He confessed also, it is said, that the accusations of Ray Schalk, Sox catcher, that Cicotte and Claude Williams double-crossed him on signals are true.

According to Attorney Austrian, Jackson made a "full, free and complete statement to Judge McDonald." After listening to his story, Judge McDonald advised him to repeat it to the grand jury, Attorney Austrian said.

Following a conference between Judge McDonald, Attorney Austrian and Jackson, Assistant State's Attorney Repogle was called and the ball player went directly to the grand jury room. He refused to talk after he had been in conference with Judge McDonald, but his lawyer said that he had decided to go before the grand jury and tell the whole truth.

"This 'blowoff' is due to Mr. Comiskey's action," said Attorney Austrian, who said that he had prepared the evidence at his client's orders, taken Cicotte to the grand jury and was adopting the same course in reference to Jackson.

"As soon as he knew what the state of affairs was he ordered me to go ahead. We rushed the evidence to the grand jury and are how having Jackson tell what he knows of the affair.

"This is due to Mr. Comiskey's desire to get at the bottom of the scandal and to have the matter cleared up at once."

The players named in the indictments are Arnold "Chick" Gandil, Fred McMullin, Oscar "Happy" Felsch, Charles "Swede" Risberg, Eddie Cicotte, Claude Williams, Joseph Jackson and George "Buck" Weaver. Gandil is the ex-member of the team.

The voting of bills against the eight players is the first time that such a thing has occurred in the history of American baseball. It follows long and costly efforts by Charles A. Comiskey, owner of the White Sox, to run down charges that his team had "thrown" the 1919 World Series—rumors which arose during the Series.

Shoeless Joe Jackson was one of the eight White Sox players banned from baseball for life by commissioner Kenesaw Mountain Landis. The debate over whether Jackson—who finished with a lifetime batting average of .356—should be allowed into the Hall of Fame continues today.

Gipp Makes a Final Appearance in Chicago

Northwestern's last conference battle was fought out this afternoon against Notre Dame's crack team. Although Notre Dame was a heavy favorite, the stands were jammed by Northwestern rooters, who witnessed their school's game stand against overwhelming odds. The cheer leaders and school bands made merry for half an hour before the opening kickoff.

Editor's Note: Notre Dame won the game by a final score of 33-7. Fighting Irish coach Knute Rockne did not intend to play George Gipp, his ailing star, but the fans chanted for their hero. Gipp finally made an appearance in the fourth quarter. He completed five of six passes for 157 yards, including touchdowns to Roger Kiley and Norm Barry. Gipp was so obviously ill that the Northwestern tacklers eased him to the ground as gently as possible whenever he carried the ball.

After the game, Gipp stayed one more day in Chicago to help a friend with a football clinic. Later that week he left the team banquet early and checked into a South Bend hospital. The All-American halfback died a few weeks later, on December 14. He was only 25. Shortly thereafter, Notre Dame wrapped up its undefeated 1920 season with a 25-0 win over Michigan Agricultural College (now Michigan State University) at East Lansing.

"I felt the thrill that comes to every coach when he knows it is his fate and his responsibility to handle unusual greatness . . . the perfect performer who comes rarely more than once in a generation."
—Knute Rockne's thoughts on George Gipp's arrival at Notre Dame

Notre Dame's George Gipp became one of college football's greatest legends.

Robertson of White Sox
Pitches Perfect Game

This is the manner in which Charley Robertson, Sherman (Tex.), pitcher for the White Sox, disposed of 27 batters in nine innings of baseball at Navin Field, Detroit, yesterday and equaled the no-hit, no-run, no-runner-on-first record that had stood for fourteen years.

First inning—Lu Blue fanned. George Cutshaw popped to Eddie Collins. Harvey McClellan threw out Ty Cobb.

Second inning—Bobby Veach flied to Johnny Mostil. Harry Heilmann lifted to Harry Hooper. Bob Jones did the same thing.

Third inning—Topper Rigney popped to Collins. Clyde Manion fouled to Ray Schalk. Herman Pillette out, McClellan to Earl Sheely.

Fourth inning—Blue fanned again. Cutshaw lined to Collins. Cobb flied to Mostil.

Fifth inning—Veach flied to Hooper. Robertson tossed out Heilmann. Jones fouled to McClellan.

Sixth inning—Rigney fouled to Sheely. Collins and Hooper got Manion. Pillette fanned.

Seventh inning—Blue was easy for Collins and Sheely. Cutshaw died, McClellan to Sheely. Cobb fanned.

Eighth inning—Veach struck out. Heilmann fouled to Sheely. Collins tossed out Jones.

Ninth inning—Danny Clark batted for Rigney and fanned. Manion popped to Collins. Johnny Bassler pinch hit for Pillette and flied to Mostil.

Comiskey picked up Robertson four years ago, but every spring when it came time for him to report he was sent to Minneapolis in the American Association. With the Millers last season Robertson won 17 games and was considered one of the steadiest pitchers in the association, despite his youthfulness and the keen competition.

In speaking of Robertson's acheivement in breaking a 14-year record, or rather equaling it from a no-hit standpoint, White Sox manager Kid Gleason said today, "In all of my 40 years in baseball I never saw anything like it, and it was the first time I ever saw a hitless game. It shows what control will do. Robertson has that, and his fast ball is a wonder. It breaks downward just enough to make heavy hitters like Cobb, Veach, Heilmann and Blue swing at the air.

Editor's Note: Robertson's perfect game in only his third major league start did not portend great things for the future. He played six more seasons in the big leagues, finishing with a career record of 49-80.

Charley Robertson

Paris Crowds Go Wild as Weissmuller Wins Race

By William E. Nash

Johnny Weissmuller of Chicago won the final heat in the 400-meter freestyle swimming race at the Olympic games today. It was an exciting race throughout. The three leaders were neck and neck over the entire distance. Arne Borg of Sweden and Weissmuller watched each other like hawks at every stroke.

The crowd of spectators was delirious with excitement, especially the Australians, who cooed wildly to encourage Charlton, the second man, whose failure to win was explained on the ground that he is an endurance athlete, like Nurmi, and not a sprinter.

Weather conditions today were most unfavorable for swimming. A cold, strong wind badly ruffled the surface of the beautiful open-air tank at Tourelles. Despite these very real handicaps, however, Weissmuller's time of 5:04.2 beat the former Olympic record in the 400-meter race.

Final results, 400-meter swim, freestyle, men: Johnny Weissmuller, Illinois A.C., first; Arne Borg, Sweden, second; Andrew Charlton, Australia, third; Ake Borg, Sweden, fourth; Hatfield, Great Britain, fifth.

Editor's Note: Weissmuller won three gold medals at the 1924 Olympics in Paris, in the 100- and 400-meter freestyle events and the 4x200-meter freestyle relay. His times of 0:59.0 in the 100 and 5:04.2 in the 400 were both Olympic records. The relay team of Weissmuller, Wallace O'Connor, Harry Glancy and Ralph Breyer set a world record with a time of 9:53.4.

At the 1928 Games in Amsterdam, Weissmuller added two more gold medals to his collection. He set a new Olympic record of 0:58.6 in winning the 100-meter freestyle. A new 4-200-meter freestyle relay team, made up of Weissmuller, Austin Clapp, Walter Laufer and George Kojac, set a new world record with a time of 9:36.2

" . . . in Austria we loved Johnny Weissmuller and his Tarzan movies. I remember when I was six years old, my father took me to see Weissmuller when he opened a swimming pool in our town."

—Arnold Schwarzenegger

After his Olympic glory, Chicago's Johnny Weissmuller went on to star in the popular Tarzan films.

Grange Successful in Debut as Professional Grid Player

Pro or amateur, Red Grange, ex-University of Illinois halfback and favorite son of Wheaton's ice buyers, is a great football player. Yesterday more than 40,000 persons jammed Cubs Park to see the famous auburn-haired runner and, while they were there, saw the Chicago Bears and Cardinals battle to a 0 to 0 tie, in as thrilling a game as ever graced a college gridiron. Grange was the cynosure of all eyes, and although he made no sensational sprints down the length of the field, he proved to the customers who had never seen him play that he is a consistent ground gainer, accurate heaver of passes and a tower of strength on defense. Grange succeeded in a brilliant manner in his debut as a paid gridiron warrior.

Red was easily the star of the contest but a good bit of praise should be showered on the heads of Paddy Driscoll and Duke Hanny. The former performed in his usual flashy style for the Cardinals and prevented Grange from running wild, even if the fans did boo his efforts. Time and time again his accurate punts sent the oval spiraling to Joe Sternaman instead of to the Wheaton flash, and although the ticket purchasers howled, "Kick it to Grange," Paddy ignored their pleas to do as he saw fit. Hanny of the Bears also came in for a share of the glory due to his wonderful punting, and in addition he played faultlessly at left end.

Although given no opportunity to reel off one of his famous 85-yard runs for a touchdown, Grange gained considerable territory for the Bears. He made 13 tries at the Cardinal line to gain a total of 36 yards. Not so bad for a man who was spotted and who was playing in a strange backfield and an unfamiliar angle of attack. The Cardinal line is not easy to penetrate either. Grange brought the fans to their feet cheering on three occasions. Driscoll was unable to direct all his kicks to Sternaman and the three that Grange caught gave him a chance to romp and he did. He returned one for 15 yards and carried the remaining two for 20 yards each. He tossed six passes which were incomplete, due mainly to the fault of the receiver. He snared the only pass completed for the Bears and intercepted a Cardinal toss on his 1-yard line to save the day for his teammates.

No official estimates were handed out as to the money received by Grange, but it is fairly safe to assume that he made the $12,000 or more for his morning's work. And he earned every cent of the amount, not only by attracting the largest crowd that ever attended a professional conflict, but also by giving the ticketholders plenty for their money. The fans came to see Grange do his stuff and he did it, even if he did not run for a touchdown.

Red Grange, "The Galloping Ghost," helped increase the popularity of the NFL when he joined the Chicago Bears after his career at the University of Illinois.

Tunney Proves Real Champion in his Defeat of Dempsey

By Robert Edgren

Jack Dempsey knocked Gene Tunney out fairly in the seventh round and lost the fight on another ten-round decision. It was the most mixed-up mess ever seen in a championship ring. As a battle it was magnificent, but the deal that was handed Dempsey smelled to heaven. Tunney was on the floor fourteen seconds and was not counted out.

Up to the seventh round it was a whale of a fight. Dempsey didn't put his head down and bore in, pounding at the body as he did with Jack Sharkey. He crouched a little and circled to Tunney's left, which made Tunney miss constantly. Every time Gene missed he rushed in and grabbed at Dempsey's arms, holding until he could get away safely. But there was no doubt Tunney looked dangerous. He was perfectly poised and moved swiftly enough to escape most of Dempsey's hardest blows.

Then came the seventh round and the sensation of the night—a sensation that brought the crowd yelling to its feet. Dempsey threw away his defense and went after Tunney like a tiger. Tunney missed left, missed with a right. He doubled back to get away. Dempsey rushed him furiously to the ropes on the west side of the ring.

Almost against the ropes, Tunney tried to get away. But Dempsey leaped at him. A terrific left hook crashed on Tunney's jaw, and Tunney was half twisted around by the blow.

He threw out his arms despairingly, trying to grab at Dempsey and hold him tight as he had held him a hundred times before.

But Dempsey's right was already on the way. It crashed on Tunney's head. Tunney didn't reel and fall. He was lifted from his feet by that second blow. He seemed to whirl in the air. He fell heavily on his back and as he struck the floor his left arm was flung across the rope.

The referee turned around toward Dempsey, who had turned uncertainly toward his corner and had not stepped into it because Tunney fell only a couple of steps from that angle of the ring. Time went by and there was no count. Then the referee bent over Tunney and after looking around toward the timekeeper he began to count slowly.

Tunney evidently needed plenty of time. At these fights I always carry a split-second watch to time knockdowns, for in the old days a favorite trick was to give a fighter a long count to save him from a knockout, especially if he was favorite in the betting. When Tunney was flat on the floor I stopped the split second hand. The count went on. Dempsey had walked away well out of range. Tunney struggled to rise and the count reached nine. Then Tunney rocked forward and came up to his feet. The referee stepped back.

As the referee counted "nine" and Tunney left the floor, I stopped the other split-second hand. According to my watch Tunney was down on his back just fourteen seconds.

In most places and under the usual run of prizering circumstances a man is out when he is knocked down and fails to rise within ten seconds. But apparently not under Chicago rules. Tunney was knocked out, but they let him go on fighting.

According to Chicago rules, the referee waits until the fighter who had delivered a knockdown reaches the farthest corner of the ring. But according to all the rules of boxing in the world, there is no excuse for giving a knocked-out fighter fourteen seconds in which to regain his feet. Tunney deserves credit for a wonderful fight after being knocked out, but many who looked on believe that Dempsey won.

Jack Dempsey stands over Gene Tunney after knocking him down in the 7th round.

Cubs Fall Short in Series

By James Crusinberry

Once more the National League has been humbled. The 1929 world series ended this afternoon when the Athletics staged a rousing ninth-inning rally that beat the struggling Cubs, 3 to 2, giving the Mackmen their fourth victory to one for the Cubs.

For eight innings Pat Malone had the American League champions licked. They hadn't scored a run and had made only two hits. On the other hand, the Cubs had batted Howard Ehmke off the rubber in the fourth and tallied two runs, after which Rube Walberg came in and stopped the McCarthy men stone still

When the ninth inning arrived and the Cubs were leading 2 to 0, the world series troopers were making ready to take a ride back to Chicago to continue things out there. But things began to happen.

It was Walberg's turn to bat for the Mackmen to start their last attack, so Walter French went up to hit for him. He fanned and that made it look easy. Max Bishop next cut a sharp hit down the third-base line, which was fair by inches and just out of Norm McMillan's reach. It didn't look dangerous, but Mule Haas changed the whole situation a moment later and sent 30,000 people into a frenzy of joy when he smacked the first pitched ball on a line drive over the right-field wall for a home run. It scored Bishop ahead of him and tied the count. Right there the affair was as good as over.

Mickey Cochrane rolled out to Rogers Hornsby, but Al Simmons, the goliath of the A's, thought there was no use in prolonging things longer. He poled a mighty double against the wall in right center. The Cubs held a conference and purposely passed Jimmie Foxx to take a chance on Bing Miller. But Malone wasn't accurate in his control and got the count of three and two. He had to put the next pitch over and Miller socked another drive almost to the same spot where Simmons had hit one, and the series was over. Simmons galloped home from second with the winning run and all the Mackmen on the bench were at the plate to hoist him into the air.

It may be that Pittsburgh fans were disappointed in the Pirates of two years ago when they lost to the Yankees in four straight games, and it may be that the same things was true a year ago when the Cardinals went down before the same team in four straight. But the biggest disappointment of all has been the Cubs of this year, even though they did win one game from the Mackmen.

The Pirates and the Cardinals were outclassed. But in this case, the general opinion is that the Cubs, fully as strong if not a stronger team than the Macks, lost because they played bad baseball.

Regardless of the fact that they suffered awful breaks in the luck of the game, the feeling still prevails that they could have won had they done what they were capable of doing.

Cubs players (left to right) Norm McMillan, Woody English, Rogers Hornsby and Charlie Grimm at Wrigley Field in 1929. The Cubs' signing of Rogers Hornsby—the Boston Braves' 1928 NL batting champ—brought to Chicago the final piece in a powerhouse lineup that drove the Cubs to the 1929 NL pennant. Hornsby responded with a .380 batting average, 39 home runs and 149 RBIs and was named the NL's MVP for 1929.

The Bears and Blackhawks matured into championship teams during the hard years of the Depression, and in the process, they helped sustain the city's spirits, with season after season of good times.

How good were the Bears? Fullback Bronko Nagurski, halfback Red Grange, end Bill Hewitt, tackles George Musso and Link Lyman and guard Danny Fortmann all landed in the Pro Football Hall of Fame, as did their owner and coach, George Halas.

The Bears suffered no losing seasons and claimed two National Football League championships during the decade. In 1934 they ran up a 13-0 regular-season record, the first such unblemished finish in NFL history.

The first title, won in December 1932, was the fruit of an unofficial championship game, played indoors at Chicago Stadium in bad weather. The Bears defeated the Portsmouth Spartans, 9-0, to finish atop the league standings and set a nearly unbreakable record by allowing just 44 points over the 14-game season, an average of just 3.3 points a game.

There was no league championship game at the time, but that would be remedied the next year. In the league's very first championship playoff, the Bears took on the New York Giants in a back-and-forth affair witnessed by 30,000 at Wrigley Field. The highlight of the day was the running and throwing of the 235-pound Nagurski. Still, the Giants held a 21-16 lead late in the fourth when Chicago took over at midfield after an errant New York punt. The Bears moved to the 32, where Nagurski passed to Bill Hewitt, who lateraled as he was about to be tackled. Chicago's Billy Karr took Hewitt's pitch and raced 25 yards for the winning score.

The momentum of that second championship carried through the undefeated regular season of 1934 and right into the third quarter of the Bears' title-game rematch with the Giants. Playing on a frozen field at the Polo Grounds in New York, Chicago moved to a 13-3 lead, which seemed safe on the nasty surface. But the Giants gave their running backs rubber-soled shoes at intermission, which allowed New York to dash off to 27 second-half points for a 30-13 win in what became known as the "sneaker game."

The Bears returned to the title game in 1937, hosting the Washington Redskins and quarterback Sammy Baugh at Wrigley Field. Baugh passed for 352 yards and three touchdowns, good enough to give the Skins a 28-21 lead. Three times in the fourth period, Nagurski, who was slowed by injuries, and the Bears bashed their way into scoring position, but Washington's defense held for the win.

The decade also brought high times for baseball, although they fell short of the ultimate prize. The Cubs returned to the World Series in 1932 to face the Yankees and Babe Ruth. Chicago fans seethed at Ruth's arrogant presence and always greeted him with boos. His response in the first inning of Game 3 was a three-run homer off pitcher Charlie Root that brought a chorus of jeers. The noise supposedly rose in waves when he came to bat again in the fifth. In the din, the Babe shouted something and waved his bat towards the Cubs' pitcher, then promptly sent one way beyond the center-field fence in Wrigley. To this day, historians still debate whether Babe's famous "called shot" was truly "called."

Beyond Chicago's World Series loss, the decade was filled with an array of classic baseball events in the Windy City, including the first All-Star Game in 1933, Hack Wilson's RBI binge in 1931, and Gabby Hartnett's "homer in the gloamin'" in 1938.

The Blackhawks, meanwhile, used the thirties to mark Chicago as a hockey town. High in the firmament of moments was Mush March's goal 30 minutes into sudden-death overtime to defeat the Detroit Red Wings in 1934 and give the Hawks their first Stanley Cup in nine years.

They did it again four years later, shoving aside the highly favored Toronto Maple Leafs, to claim the 1938 Stanley Cup.

As Chicagoans battled the Great Depression in America and Europeans were faced with the rising power of Germany's Adolf Hitler, the most important sporting event of the 1930s was taking place at the 1936 Olympics in Berlin. At the games, Hitler's Aryan myth was shattered by the medal-winning performances of American sprinters Jesse Owens (left) and Chicago native Ralph Metcalfe (center), who were joined on the United States sprint team by Frank Mykoff (right). Rewriting the record books, Owens won an unprecedented four gold medals and Metcalfe captured a gold and silver. Metcalfe later distinguished himself off the track as a prominent businessman and local politician, serving first on the Chicago City Council and then as a U.S. congressman from Illinois.

Cubs Beat Reds, 13-8

By James Crusinberry

Hornsby's Cubs won a practice game today from the Cincinnati Reds. They were practicing swinging bats, and knocked the ball all over the place, winning 13 to 8. The idea was to get themselves into great batting form for the coming series with the Sox, as the game today meant nothing.

The heavy swinging of Hack Wilson and Gabby Hartnett was the feature. Each of these sluggers added two home runs to their season's total, making 56 for Hack and 37 for Gabby. The sluggers knocked Ray Kolp off the mound in the fourth and Eppa Rixey took his place and finished the game. Pat Malone pitched for the Cubs and turned in his 20th win of the season.

Editor's Note: On September 28, in the last game of the season, the Cubs beat the Reds 13-11. Wilson went 2-for-3 and drove in two runs, bringing his season RBI total to 190. In 1999, Wilson's RBI total was officially changed to 191, as noted in this June 22 press release from Major League Baseball.

"Following an exhaustive review of box scores and play-by-play accounts of the National League's 1930 season, Hack Wilson's single-season major league record for RBI[s] has been adjusted from 190 to 191, Baseball Commissioner Allan H. (Bud) Selig announced today.

"Wilson's missing RBI was officially confirmed last week when a committee led by Jerome Holtzman, Major League Baseball's Official Historian, examined the issue.

"'There is no doubt that Hack Wilson's RBI total should be 191,' Commissioner Selig said. 'I am sensitive to the historical significance that accompanies the correction of such a prestigious record, especially after so many years have passed, but it is important to get it right.'

"The discrepancy in Wilson's RBI record stems from the second game of a doubleheader between the Cincinnati Reds and Chicago Cubs at Wrigley Field on July 28, 1930. Wilson was not credited with an RBI in that game, which the Cubs won, 5-3, on the strength of a four-run third inning rally. The official scorer credited Cubs first baseman Charlie Grimm with two RBI[s] and Wilson with none.

"The Associated Press box score credited both Grimm and Wilson with one RBI each. In addition, play-by-play reports and game stories from the *Chicago Tribune, Chicago Daily News, Chicago Daily Times* and the *Chicago Herald-Examiner* clearly stated that Wilson drove in a third-inning run.

"A partial play-by-play account of the Cubs' third-inning rally states: 'Blair singled to center. English singled, sending Blair to third, and took second on Heilmann's throw to third. Cuyler doubled, scoring Blair and English. Wilson singled, scoring Cuyler.'"

Over the years, Lou Gehrig has come the closest to breaking Wilson's record, driving in 184 runs in 1931. Since 1950, the nearest challenge has come from Cleveland's Manny Ramirez, who drove in 165 runs in 1999.

Hack Wilson gave the Cubs of the 1930s record-setting production at the plate.

Yanks, Ruth Toast Wrigley

By Robert J. Casey

In a field which after the unexplored reaches of Yankee Stadium looked like nothing so much as a tennis court, the Chicago Cubs assembled today to find out whether or not the so-called world's series is really over.

They received boisterous encouragement from the bleacher crowds, most of whom were sitting in the outfielders' laps or else in the middle of Sheffield Avenue. Despite early indications that the dollar-ten-cent market was going a trifle sour, this section of the stands was well filled an hour before game time, making the vast green emptiness of the reserved sections seem lonelier by contrast.

The bleachers were given promise of a profitable day as soon as the Yanks came up for their batting practice. Young Mr. Babe Ruth, experimenting with a right field that can be seen without the aid of binoculars, dropped three or four balls into the laps of the long-distance customers and then fooled them by putting the next one clear over the top tier of bleachers and across Sheffield Avenue to some point near the unprotected "L" structure.

The stands began to fill up somewhat around 1 o'clock and bright dresses and light overcoats and hats gave color to an otherwise drab and uninteresting vista. The numerous ushers in blue and gold uniforms made whole sections of the stands look like flower beds in movement, while the caps of the wandering refreshment purveyors did their bit to provide pleasing contrast.

At the end of four innings, the score was tied 4 to 4. Mr. Joe Sewell opened the fifth for the Yanks and went out on a close play at first. The next batter, Mr. Ruth, drew a strike and was cheered. He let a ball go by and was booed. Came another ball and more disturbance. He let another strike go by and was cheered. Whereupon he stuck a home run through the scoreboard opening beyond the center field fence. Mr. Lou Gehrig, greatest of all ersatz Ruth, hit the next ball pitched for another home run just inside the flag pole at the right-field corner.

The Yankees won the game 7 to 5, and now lead the series three games to none.

Editor's Note: Did Babe Ruth really call his homer in the 5th inning? This much we know. The Babe and the Cubs' players had been feuding during most of the world series, and the feud seemed to intensify during Ruth's 5th-inning at bat. But when Ruth gestured with his arm from the batter's box, was he pointing his finger at Cubs pitcher Charlie Root? Or was he hollering at the Cubs' bench? Or was he in fact pointing to the center-field bleachers? Ruth denied in his 1948 autobiography that he "called" his shot, but the fact remains that the very next pitch from Root sailed over the center-field wall. And so the debate rages on.

Fact or fiction? Babe Ruth's home run in the 1932 World Series is the source of the "called shot" controversy. Speculation continues today over whether Ruth really pointed to the bleachers or whether the story is merely a baseball legend.

Chicago's Comiskey Park Hosts Baseball's Inaugural All-Star Clash

By John P. Carmichael

They were still the All-Americans at the halfway point.

Out in Comiskey Park, in the presence of 29,000 fans, with the sun beating down from a cloudless sky, the marionettes of Connie Mack led the minions of John J. McGraw with more than half a game yet to go.

One mighty sweep of his bat and a hunch of those powerful shoulders and Babe Ruth, the Yankee behemoth, sent one of Wild Bill Hallahan's floaters far out there into the right-field bleachers and strolled around those sacks behind Charlie Gehringer, as the thousands roared their "bravos" and stretched their hands in a vain effort to bridge the gap from the grandstand to the diamond.

Picked teams of the National and American leagues met in battle today for the first time in baseball history. The game was sponsored by the Chicago Tribune.

"Wild Bill" stayed around for one more man, and then passed from the spotlight of this game of the century, as from the bullpen out yonder came Lonnie Warneke, the big train of the Cubs, to force Al Simmons to hit into a double play and keep the National Leaguers in the game.

Everywhere was a riot of color and the glamour and excitement of a holiday.

One after another, the stars of the greatest teams in baseball trudged their way to the batting box and received their ovations. Above all, the shrill cries of the hawkers and the slow and measured voice of the park announcer cut their way.

Came a pause at the end of the four and one-half innings and a switch in the baseballs and umpires. Umpire Bill Klem, the dean of the National League

arbiters, took the place of Bill Dineen behind the plate while the slower and heavier National League ball was tossed into the fray. It was all conducted according to Hoyle, this game of games.

Out in the bullpens, the two greatest southpaws in baseball suddenly got to their feet and began to limber up. Along the right-field foul line Carl Hubbell, the ace of the Giants, worked out with the Cubs' Gabby Hartnett receiving. Far down on the left-field line, Robert Moses Grove, the speed-ball king of the American League, flipped his preliminary offerings to a number of receivers.

Up strode Lou Gehrig to the plate in the fifth inning, with Babe Ruth on the bases. The arm of Warneke rose and fell, as Larrupin' Lou swung three times and missed and went back to his dugout, a sadder and wiser man. The stands cheered Lou to the echo for that feature.

Up came Warneke to the plate in the sixth inning, with a man already dead, and smote himself a triple that drove Ruth crazy out there in right field. Home he came a minute later on an infield out, with the first run that this National League had been able to get off either Lefty Gomez or Gen. Alvin Crowder of the pacemaking Senators.

The roar of welcome that he received had hardly died away before the diminutive figure of Frankie Frisch was racing around the base lines, as the ball from his bat was arching into the right field stands. The National Leaguers were back in the ball game, even though Chick Hafey, the Reds' star gardener, was thrown out by Jimmy Dykes. Two runs!

Babe Ruth homered at Comiskey Park to propel the American League to a 4-2 victory over the National League in baseball's first All-Star game.

Old Storybook Finish
Wins Pro Title for Bears

By Howard Roberts

Trot out all the pretty adjectives and superlatives you can find in Noah Webster's noted tome, polish them up and present them to Chicago's champion Bears. They deserve them.

Even then, you can't possibly do justice to those amazing Bears and the hysterical, breathtaking, almost unbelievable 23-21 triumph they scored over the New York Giants yesterday to retain their scepter as champions of professional football.

Throughout the season the Bears have won renown for their never-say-die spirit and stirring fourth-quarter rallies. But never did they rise to the heights they attained yesterday when they fought their way from behind three times for the most amazing of all the storybook finishes.

Confronted with as perfect a pass attack as any team ever unleashed, the Bears were forced to respond with brilliant passes of their own. These, combined with three field goals from placement from the toe of "Automatic" Jack Manders, enabled them to turn the tide.

Hailed as the greatest offensive teams in football, the title rivals didn't waste any time in proving it, despite the handicap of a field that was quite slippery, especially on the grassy part that had been unprotected by tarpaulin. The Bears seemed to have an edge in the play, but they wound up with a 7-6 deficit at the end of the half.

At the start of the third period, the Bears launched a drive that ended in a third Manders field goal. Two nice runs by Bronko Nagurski and a 27-yard pass from George Corbett to Carl Brumbaugh carried the ball deep into New York territory, Manders booting the ball over from the 18-yard line.

The Giants struck back through the air with a dazzling array of passes. Harry Newman threw one to Dale Burnett, another to Burnett, then one to Kink Richards. Next, he tossed a shovel pass to Red Badgro and followed with a forward to Max Krause, who was run outside a yard from the Bear goal line. Richards failed to gain, but on the next play, Krause hit the middle of the line for a touchdown. Ken Strong added the point.

That put the Giants ahead 14-9, but only for about three minutes. Corbett hustled the kickoff back 23 yards, and on third down he tossed a pass to Brumbaugh, who caught the ball near midfield and, by a beautiful twisting run, advanced 67 yards to the Giant 8-yard line. Two plays netted two yards. Then Nagurski faked a plunge at center and pitched a short pass to Bill Karr, who caught it in the end zone for a touchdown. Not a Giant was near him. Manders added the point.

Trailing 16-14, the Giants again called on Newman's passing skill, and again he responded with an astounding exhibition of accuracy. Three successive tosses netted 59 yards, and Strong then picked up 14 through the line. Again Newman passed, this one to Burnett for eight, and the ball was inside the Bear 10-yard stripe. Strong swung wide to his left and, just as he was about to be tackled, pitched the ball laterally to Newman, who reversed his field, dodging beautifully. Then, as two Bear tacklers launched themselves at him, he passed to Strong, who fell over for a touchdown. Strong also added the point, and the Giants led 21-16.

Still the Bears refused to admit defeat. Following an exchange of punts, a pass from Keith Molesworth to Brumbaugh took the ball to the Giant 36-yard line. Nagurski picked up four at center, then shot a pass over the line to Bill Hewitt, who tossed a lateral to Karr. Behind some fine blocking by Gene Ronzani, Karr winged his way down the sideline for the winning touchdown. Manders kicked the point for the final tally.

Bronko Nagurski led the Bears to back-to-back championships in 1932 and 1933.

Blackhawks March to 1st Stanley Cup

By Gene Kessler

He's short and dumpy and as fast as greased lightning. Today he's the toast of a hockey-minded Chicago.

This atom of the ice is Harold (Mush) March and his goal after 30 minutes and 5 seconds of sudden death overtime gave the Blackhawks the world's championship and sent 16,800 yodelers home from the Stadium last night chortling with enough mirth to last until the next hockey season.

It gave the Hawks their first Stanley Cup in nine years of strenuous campaigning. And, at conclusion of that tense, throbbing battle last night, Hawk players celebrated right there on the frost.

Maj. Frederic McLaughlin, owner of the club, put an armlock on the ancient trophy, presented to him by president Frank Calder of the league, and stood there in the midst of a wild hurrah by a gang of tired hockey players. The major smiled and accepted congratulations from his neighbor, Big Jim Norris, Chicago broker who owns the Detroit Red Wings.

Norris' Wings had fought these champion Hawks for 90 minutes before losing that final series, 3 games to 1.

The Musher scored two goals during the entire play-off competition. His first beat Les Canadiens in a sudden-death overtime session and kept the Hawks in the running. His second last night won the title, beating the Wings, 1 to 0.

It was a killing pace, this ice battle last night. Starting cautiously and so tensely their muscles knotted, the players gradually opened the throttle until the last regulations period was a whirling, incessant hailstorm of action.

During this time, the Hawks held an edge. They were doing all the pressing, bearing down and checking back savagely. They back-checked and bumped these Wings out of most rushes. Occasionally that buzz-saw, Larry Aurie, and Herbie Lewis swarmed down like bees and rattled shots off Chuck Gardiner's pads and stick. Chuck was on his toes last night, playing his usual great game in the net and proving to the gallery boys who had greeted him with boos that he can take it.

For a time it looked like the hockey endurance record of 1 hour and 4 minutes of overtime was in danger. Then came the dramatic ending. Ebbie Goodfellow hunched over the penalty seat to cool off for tripping Tom Cook at the 9-minute mark of the second overtime session.

Three times these Wings repulsed the Hawks on pressure plays. And then Doc Romnes impinged Lewis against the north boards in Detroit territory. Doc maneuvered the puck away from Cooney Weiland on the face-off, handed the overgrown chip to March and the Musher did the rest.

Mush streaked along the boards and fired a backhanded flip from a side angle. It whizzed off goalie Wilf Cude's shirt into the opposite corner of the net, igniting the final red light of the season—the one which blocked all hockey traffic for the Blackhawks.

That the Hawks were back-checking is shown in figures. Cude made 53 stops and Gardiner only 39 in 90 minutes of pulsating hockey.

Only three penalties were called during this championship battle, although both teams body-checked violently. Two were called in the opening few minutes, one on Marker of the Wings and another on Rosie Couture of the Hawks. The other was Goodfellow's sentence in that sudden-death overtime, and it was a fatal one for the Wings.

Big Train Conacher saved the title for the Hawks during the third period when Hap Emms' shot hit Gardiner on the Adam's apple and dazed him for a few minutes. Chuck fell, but missed the puck, and Conacher beat the Wings to it.

Tommy Cook, Roger Jenkins, Leroy Goldsworthy and Lionel Conacher (left to right) were all members of the Blackhawks' first Stanley Cup-winning squad.

Bomber Beats Jim Braddock
in 8 Hot Rounds

By John P. Carmichael

Death came to the champion. He lay on his right side where he fell on the light-drenched canvas, face pillowed in an ever-widening pool of his own blood, while in the far corner his killer stood with eyes averted from the spectacle which tugged at 55,000 hearts. The timekeeper's toll fell on unheeding ears. So did the roar of the multitude, reverberating through Comiskey Park.

Soon . . . so soon . . . it was all official and the remains of James J. Braddock were borne to the corner wherein he sat, half an hour earlier, as champion of the world. And then Joe Louis, the boy who would be king, ascended the throne which no colored man has graced since the days of Jack Johnson. Today, at 23, he rules as the youngest titleholder ever to head boxing's mightiest division, with a European continent beckoning his pleasure.

He got up off the floor to come on and win. Dropped in the first round by a right smash to the body, the Brown Bomber picked himself up so quickly as to preclude even a count of "one" and exacted a terrible penalty from a gallant Irishman. He forced Braddock to miss. He wore Jim down and watched the steam ooze out of the champion's blows. He punched red sores below both of Jim's eyes. He cut open one eye at the corner and the nose and cut about his left ear at the finish. Jim didn't try to stay away. He didn't leave his crown in the dressing room. He wore it as a chip on his shoulder

and dared Louis, with every gesture, to knock it off. Joe did. He was 2-1 to do so and, once he had weathered the first four rounds, when it looked as though he was in distress on several occasions, he won on a 10-1 shot.

Braddock obviously was "short," as they say at the track. He was rusty. On top of that he was facing a killer who was determined to beat his way back from semi-obscurity to which a knockout by Max Schmeling had consigned him. Superbly conditioned and coached to block the left hooks and right crosses with which Braddock might hope to wear him down, Louis looked the part of a champion.

Jim landed the first blow as they came out fighting and Louis the last, eight rounds later. In between, punishment was constant and clinches of short duration. Right to the end, Louis respected Braddock's flagging efforts to turn the tide of battle.

Louis fought a smart fight, probably the best defensive battle he ever has waged. But then Louis never had to pay much attention to defense. This time he wasn't the vicious animal that struck terror to the hearts of King Levinksy, Max Baer, Primo Carnera and others of that ilk, but he was a more finished workman. He knew from the first minute that Braddock intended to carry the fight, and forewarned was forearmed. Louis merely bided his time and caught the champion trying to extend himself beyond the bounds of endurance.

Joe Louis and Jim Braddock receive their final instructions before their historic bout. Billed as "A Night to Remember," historians note that while the Louis-Braddock fight was underway, Benny Goodman's band was performing to a packed crowd at the 8th Regiment Armory only a short walk down the road from Comiskey Park. Just a year earlier, Goodman had become the first white bandleader to include black musicians in his ensemble. After the fight, bedlam erupted when Louis and his entourage walked into the Armory and joined the cheering throngs enjoying the swing sounds of Goodman's band, which included two of America's greatest jazz musicians, Teddy Wilson and Lionel Hampton.

It's De Correvont's Day: 90,000 . . . 26-0

By Frank Muskrat

It was "S.R.O." at Soldier Field yesterday. In fact, the largest crowd—90,000—ever to see a high school football game watched Austin pound the lighter but courageous Leo club, 26 to 0, to capture the city prep grid title. Austin is public school champion, Leo, the Catholic league titlist. Together they now hold the world's championship for drawing high school crowds.

As usual, it was a personal triumph for Austin's Bill De Correvont, who scored three touchdowns and passed to teammate Sanford Skor for the fourth.

Every good seat in the stadium was filled long before game time, and at the end of the first quarter the crowd standing along the edges of the stands broke away and formed a horseshoe around the playing field.

Ultimate winners are Chicago's needy children. Proceeds of the game go into the coffers of Mayor Kelly's Christmas benefit fund for the city's needy children, an annual institution since Mayor Kelly conceived the event in 1934.

So widespread was the fame of Austin's De Correvont—he cracked the prep scoring record this year with 30 touchdowns—he literally stacked 'em in. Johnny Galvin, Leo's right-handed passer, likewise drew his quota of fans.

Leo put up a surprisingly strong defense, but the superior weight of Austin—Leo was outweighed 15 pounds to the man—began to tell in the second period, and Austin surged on to score twice in the second, once in the third, and added the final counter in the closing period.

In the first period the teams scrapped cautiously, stabbing at the line and waiting for the breaks. Tom Martin, of Leo, speared a De Correvont pass on Leo's 20 to break up a scoring threat, and Warren McLaughlin intercepted another on the 10-yard line.

Jack Daley broke off right end for a 35-yard run, the longest of the period. Leo got a break when Galvin's punt struck an official and was grounded on Austin's 2-yard line, and Galvin returned the ensuing punt 22 yards to Austin's 14. The Leo drive bogged down and Austin took the ball on downs on its 9.

In the second period, after an exchange of punts, De Correvont faked an end sweep, cut back over right tackle, and set sail for the goal line 48 yards away. He swiveled through the entire Leo line for the first score.

Austin turned on the power in the same period, Skor and Peifer relieving De Correvont and inching to the 1-yard line. De Correvont dived over for his second counter. Bauman kicked goal.

Leo threw caution to the winds in the last half, but could not maneuver into scoring position. De Correvont tried a field goal from his 30, but the kick fell short. Austin drove again to the 3-yard line, and De Correvont sliced off right tackle for No. 3. Bauman's kick was low.

The last period found Leo gambling desperately, but the odds were too great. Austin's weight slowly surged the fighting Leo line back, and De Correvont flung a 15-yard pass to Skor, who was standing in the end zone, for the final counter.

Gordon McKenzie, substitute guard, attempted a drop-kick but was wide. That ended the scoring for the day, but Leo never stopped fighting until the final whistle.

After his stellar career at Chicago's Austin High School, Bill De Correvont went on to play college football at Northwestern University. After college, he played five seasons in the NFL, where he was used as both an offensive back and a defensive back, as well as a punt and kickoff returner. De Correvont spent 1945 with the Washington Redskins and 1946 with the Detroit Lions. In 1947, he was a member of the Chicago Cardinals' championship squad. His last two years (1948 and 1949) were spent with the Chicago Bears. In his NFL career, De Correvont compiled 233 yards rushing, 417 yards receiving, 248 yards on punt returns, 655 yards on kickoff returns, three touchdowns and 10 interceptions.

Hawks Beat Leafs at Own Game to Win Stanley Cup

By Bob Stanton

"We'll beat them at their own game, whichever game they want to play, clean or rough," said the Blackhawks as they skated out to meet their enemies, the Toronto Maple Leafs, last night.

And they did. They beat them at body checking, they beat them at high-sticking, and, incidentally, they beat them at scoring goals, a department of the game which has been at times overshadowed in public attention by fisticuffs since the beginning of the finals in the Stanley Cup playoffs.

They beat them at straight hockey, and so stand today as the most sensational winners of that cup in ice history, and the most astounding upsetters of sport dope since the lowly Boston baseball Braves whipped the mighty Athletics in the world series, four to zero, 24 years ago.

The Leafs, in betting odds, had been a 4 to 1 favorite to sweep the Hawks into the discard, but the Chicago team, rising on the wings of some incredible spirit and determination, whipped their powerful opponents three games out of four, and by the one-sided score of 4 to 1 in the final game. Experts believe that if their regular goaltender, Mike Karakas, had been able to play in the second game of the series, the Hawks would have won three straight.

And the victory which thrilled the Hawks almost as much as their winning of the cup was the reduction of their personal enemy, Red Horner, Leaf captain, to docility. The big Leaf defense man, who played without his proverbial skill or spirit in this last game, limped off toward the dressing room at the end, too dejected to join his teammates in congratulations to the new champions.

The Hawks scored in every period to win the championship. Cully Dahlstrom was the first to tally on a poke shot of a rebound from the stick of Jack Shill. Goalie Turk Broda was sprawled on the ice as the puck bounced into the cage at 5:52.

Less than three minutes later the Leafs tied the score when Gordon Drillon took a pass from Jimmy Fowler and beat Mike Karakas on a 10-foot shot.

The Hawks took the lead in the second period and put the game on ice. Carl Voss shook off defensemen Reg Hamilton and Fowler 10 feet from the net and sank a rifle shot in 16:45. Johnny Gottselig and Rog Jenkins were awarded assists on the play.

At 17:58 Jack Shill decided to drop hockey and show the throng some golf. Standing near the Hawk blue line, Shill sent a mashie to the green, and while Broda stood in amazement, the disc skittered between his legs and the red light winked.

Mush March scored his third-period goal on a pass from Doc Romnes with less than four minutes remaining before the final siren. But before his tall goalie Karakas gave a great exhibition of net-minding when the entire Leaf team with the exception of Broda ganged on the Hawk cage in successive waves of desperation.

The Blackhawks celebrate their surprise Stanley Cup win over the Toronto Maple Leafs. The enormity of the Blackhawks' upset is best reflected in their rather dismal regular-season record of 14-25-9 and the fact that they had beaten Toronto only once in six tries during the season. So unlikely was Chicago's victory that the Stanley Cup was still in Toronto when the Hawks clinched the title in Chicago.

Hartnett's Homer Puts Cubs in 1st Place

By Howard Roberts

A home run, arching from the bat of old Gabby Hartnett with two out in the ninth inning and the count two strikes and no balls this afternoon put a fitting climax to one of the most dramatic baseball games of history, and lifted the Cubs to a 6 to 5 victory over the prostrate forms of these same Pirates from Pittsburgh.

Darkness was settling deep over Wrigley Field when Old Gabby swung. The umpires were preparing to call the game. They didn't have to, for the ball, rising gradually on a long line, was vanishing among the fans in the left-field bleachers almost before a spontaneous roar burst from the throats of 34,465 fans.

Gabby, trotting calmly when he felt like prancing, picked up a convoy of fans as he rounded first. By the time he had reached second he was joined by more fans, a few ushers and an escort of hysterical teammates. "Dizzy" Dean, hopping up and down like a madman and waving his arms like a windmill, met him at third, and between third and home the crowd was so dense Hartnett didn't have to trot—he was swept along.

Thus was the perfect ending written to a ball game packed with thrills and heartbreaks—a game which saw the Cubs take the lead, lose it, tie it up, fall behind again and then tie it up in an almost equally dramatic manner.

That tie, and Gabby's subsequent heroics, were made possible by additional heroics by another old-timer—Tony Lazzeri. Old Tony emerged from the obscurity of the dugout, where he has languished for many weeks, to crash out a double in the eighth inning to erase a two-run Pirate lead acquired in the same frame.

The winning pitcher appropriately was another old Cub hero—Charlie Root. Grizzled Charlie took up the mound chores in the ninth, the sixth Cub pitcher to see duty, and blanked the Bucs in short order even though annoyed by a single. The loser was Mace Brown, third Pirate hurler.

And so the Cubs, in first place for the first time since June 8 when the Giants knocked them off the top rung, face the Pirates again tomorrow in the series final with a chance to widen their lead to a game and a half. Bill Lee, ace of the staff, will pitch for the fourth consecutive day. His opponent will be Russ Bauers.

Editor's Note: Gabby Hartnett's ninth-inning, two out, two-strike "homer in the gloamin'" was part of the Cubs' incredible 20-3 finish to the 1938 season that allowed them to jump over Pittsburgh, New York and Cincinnati in the NL pennant race. Three days after Hartnett's big blast, the Cubs clinched the pennant and advanced to the World Series to take on the Yankees, who swept the Cubs in four games. The Cubs' World Series curse beats on.

Catcher Gabby Hartnett took his place in Cubs lore with his "homer in the gloamin'."

The United States would soon find itself in the thick of a world war that would change everything. There were rationing limits on rubber and other products, and team rosters were thinned by athletes rushing into combat. But Chicago's sports teams somehow managed to boost spirits on the home front.

Mostly they did it by winning.

The Bears won three titles, beginning with that 73-0 smashing of the Redskins in the 1940 NFL title game. Then came another title in 1941, when Halas' bunch set a league record by averaging 36 points a game. They lost to the Redskins, 14-6, in the 1942 championship bout, but claimed another trophy in 1943, despite the fact that Halas himself had gone into the service. The fourth title came in '46, a 24-14 dismissal of the Giants at the Polo Grounds before an NFL-record crowd of 58,346.

When the Bears finally wearied of winning it all, the Chicago Cardinals proved worthy of the task, taking the 1947 championship, 28-21, over the Philadelphia Eagles.

The Irish, meanwhile, were busy racking up their own good times. Notre Dame officials were seeking another Knute Rockne when they hired Frank Leahy to run their football program in 1941. From the perspective of history, it seems they got that and more. Rockne's winning percentage was slightly better. But in 11 seasons, Leahy gave the Golden Dome six undefeated seasons, five national championships, four Heisman Trophy winners, and another grand chapter in the Irish book of legends.

In1943, when the Irish finished at 9-1 and were the unanimous choice as national champions, the Northwestern Wildcats, with Otto Graham, also rose into the Top 10.

It was also the decade that basketball found a home in Chicago, with the success of De Paul and George Mikan in the National Invitational Tournament, and with the emergence of the Globetrotters as the major drawing card of pro basketball. Their name said Harlem, but they were pure Chicago.

In 1939, the *Chicago Herald-American* began sponsorship of a pro tourney that ran for the next decade. Played in Chicago Stadium, the tournament drew 12 to 16 teams each year from the various league champions and top barnstorming teams of that era before the NBA. In some years the crowds reached 20,000, and the pro players considered it the event that settled their championship.

The Globetrotters had gotten their start in Chicago in the twenties as the Savoy Big Five, playing out of Chicago's Savoy Ballroom. But they were merely a regional team then. It would take more than a decade before they began to garner "global" attention, competing in Chicago's World Tournament.

In later years, they would become known for their humorous routines and slick ball-handling, often performed to the accompaniment of "Sweet Georgia Brown." But in the early days, the Globetrotters played their basketball straight. The entertainment and humor were said to be a means of deflecting the ugly racial moods the team sometimes encountered on the road. Plus, if the local teams had fun and the crowd laughed, people didn't mind losing, and the Globetrotters were often invited back.

In the 1940s, Saperstein signed two stars. Reece "Goose" Tatum, a baseball player from Arkansas, had huge hands, long arms and a wonderful wit. And when Oklahoma's Langston University team beat the Trotters, Saperstein promptly lured away the star player, Marques Haynes. Building on Tatum's creativity, the Globetrotters left the straight game to offer fans their hugely entertaining brand of hoops, filled with gimmicks, gags and top-notch ballhandling.

Today, the Trotters are recognized as the world's greatest ambassadors for the game of basketball.

Luke Appling of the White Sox and Joe DiMaggio of the Yankees were just two of the many players whose baseball careers were interrupted when they answered their country's call to service during World War II.

Bears Beat Redskins, 73-0

By Howard Roberts

The Bears are rolling homeward today as the new monarchs of the football world and no champions ever had a better right to the throne.

In whipping Washington 73-0 yesterday they divided their 11 touchdowns among 10 men, Harry Clark getting a pair and Gary Famiglietti, Bill Osmanski, Ken Kavanaugh, Joe Maniaci, Sid Luckman, Bulldog Turner, Ray Nolting, George McAfee and Hampton Pool one each. In all, 16 Bears shared in the point production, the extra-point conversions going to Jack Manders, Phil Martinovich, Bob Snyder (2), Dick Plasman and Joe Stydahar on kicks and Maniaci adding one on a pass from Snyder just for variety.

They earned 372 yards by rushing while holding the Redskins to a mere three yards and, in all, they gained 492 yards.

They intercepted eight of the famed Washington passes, three of them touchdowns.

Thus were the Bears avenged for two previous upsets at the hands of the Redskins who beat them in the playoff of 1937 by 28-21 and then, three weeks ago, nosed out the Bears, 7-3.

The Bears were out in front with a touchdown lead before most of the crowd had settled into their seats after the opening kickoff, which Nolting returned 23 yards to the Bears' 26. McAfee knifed over left tackle for six and then came the explosion. Osmanski took a lateral from Luckman, raced for the sideline, then cut down field with a burst of speed that carried him over, Manders converting.

Osmanski again broke up the party, this time with a 23-yard jaunt that started a parade of power that car-

ried the length of the field, with Luckman picking up the final half a yard with a quarterback sneak. Snyder kicked the point.

George Musso partially blocked Sammy Baugh's punt, then Maniaci swung wide on the same play that broke Osmanski loose and galloped down the sideline for a touchdown. Martinovich kicked the point to make it 21-0 at the quarter.

The fourth score arrived late in the second quarter when Kavanaugh made a nice catch of Luckman's 30-yard pass in the end zone. It was then Snyder's turn to make the point and he did.

Early in the third period Pool reached up to pull down Baugh's flat pass intended for Jimmy Johnston. There was no one to annoy him as he ran 15 yards for the touchdown. Plasman converted.

Soon after Nolting ran 11 yards and then 23 to the goal line, no one laying a hand on him. Plasman missed his kick. Next McAfee intercepted Roy Zimmerman's pass and sped 34 yards for a touchdown. Stydahar kicked goal.

Turner intercepted a Zimmerman pass and ran 20 yards to score, after which Maniaci's kick was blocked. In the final quarter Clark sprinted 42 yards on a "keep it" play and Famiglietti converted.

Frankie Filchock, back to pass, fumbled and Jack Torrance recovered on the Washington 2-yard line. Famiglietti crashed over and for variety, Sherman passed to Maniaci for the point.

Clark romped over from the 1-yard line to climax a march from the midfield.

After guiding the Bears to NFL championships in 1940 and 1941, and a runner-up finish in 1942, Bears coach George Halas entered the service in 1943. That didn't stop the Bears, who captured the 1943 title in his absence.

Chicago Sees Satchel Paige Star in Negro Classic

By Bob Tatar

Negro baseball's No. 1 hero—pitcher Leroy "Satchel" Paige of the Kansas City Monarchs—drum-majored the Western team to a spectacular 2 to 1 victory over the Eastern representatives to terminate the East's three-year reign in the 11th annual Negro All-Star baseball classic yesterday. A crowd of 51,723, the largest gathering that has witnessed a ball game in Chicago in the past two seasons, jammed Comiskey Park, the scene of hostilities, to capacity. It was estimated that another 10,000 prospective customers were turned away.

Paige pitched the first three innings for the West and was as invincible as ever. He was obliged to hurl to only 10 batters. Over the span, the slender pitching star retired four men on strikes and permitted only one man to get on base. He walked Josh Gibson of the Homesteads to open the second frame and the East's catcher reached second base on a passed ball. No East player was able to advance as far as second base again, until the ninth inning uprising against pitcher Theolic Smith of Cleveland.

Buck Leonard of the Washington Homestead Grays smashed a home run into the right field bleachers, with the bases barren and two away, to save the East from the humiliation of a shutout in the ninth. Gibson and Howard Easterling of the Homesteads followed with singles and the West's cause began to look dark, indeed.

However, Smith was replaced hastily by Porter Moss of the Memphis Red Sox.

Manager Vic Harris of the East team, also from the Homesteads, batted for Lennie Pearson. His best was a long fly to Willard Brown of the Kansas City Monarchs, which ended the game.

Paige gained credit for the victory when his mates presented him with a run in the second inning. Neil Robinson reached first on a walk to open the inning, went to second on Johnny O'Neil's bounder to pitcher Dave Barnhill and scored on the first hit of the game—a single to right by Tommy Sampson.

"Lefty" McKinnis of Birmingham followed Paige on the mound for the next three innings, and was just as effective as his predecessor, although he yielded the East its first hit—a single to Horacio Martinez in the sixth.

It was during McKinnis' span on the mound that the West put over what proved to be the winning run. Brown singled to start the fourth, stole second, went to third on an infield out and scored on O'Neil's bounder to pitcher John Wright.

Smith went in to pitch for the West in the seventh, and it looked like a one-hit feat for the victors until he ran into trouble with two gone in the ninth.

Satchel Paige

Mikan May Be Out of Lineup Tonight

De Paul faced the possibility of battling Bowling Green of Ohio for the National Invitational basketball championship here tonight without the services of George Mikan, the Demons' 6-foot 9-inch All-America center.

Mikan has been taking heat treatments for a muscle injury on the calf of his left leg incurred last week and hopes to play although he may be unable to realize his full effectiveness. Without him De Paul would be no better than an even money choice to win the title.

Tuesday night New York University, which vanquished Ohio State 70-65 in an overtime Saturday for the Eastern division crown, meets Oklahoma A&M, the Western winner, for the NCAA title here. The victor opposes the De Paul-Bowling Green winner on Thursday in a Red Cross benefit game for the mythical national championship.

Editor's Note: Mikan did play in the National Invitational championship game, scoring 34 points as the Blue Demons defeated Bowling Green 71-54 at Madison Square Garden. He averaged 40 points per game in De Paul's three NIT victories, tallying 33 against West Virginia and 53 against Rhode Island. After graduating from college he played for the Minneapolis Lakers and led them to five NBA championships in six years.

"We would set up a zone defense that had four men around the key and I guarded the basket. When the other team took a shot, I'd just go up and tap it out."

—George Mikan explaining De Paul's defensive scheme. This strategy forced the NCAA to outlaw what is now known as goaltending.

De Paul sensation George Mikan went on to a stellar NBA career, winning five championships with the Minneapolis Lakers. After his NBA career, he became the first commissioner of the American Basketball Association.

Cubs Beat Bucs, 4-3; Clinch Flag!

By Herbert Simons

Both teams started fast, scoring one run each in the opening inning, as the Cubs and Pirates clashed in the opener of their pennant-hinged doubleheader here this afternoon.

Scoring recipes were virtually identical in both instances, high men in the batting order furnishing the power.

The Cubs won, 4-3, to clinch the National League pennant. Hank Borowy was batted off the Cubs' hill in the ninth as the Pirates threatened seriously.

Stan Hack opened the Cub first with a double, went to third when Roy Hughes beat out an infield roller and scored on Peanuts Lowrey's long fly to center. Then Al Gionfriddo opened the Pittsburgh first with a two-baser and scored on Johnny Barrett's single immediately afterward.

Rain which fell throughout the morning started again in the second inning, but the teams played on nevertheless in a concerted effort to avert a postponement which would shoo the Cubs into the pennant without a struggle.

Neither team scored through the second, third and fourth frames, but the Cubs moved back in front, 2-1, in the fifth with a run made possible largely through Frank Gustine's wild throw to first.

Len Merullo walked to start the Cubs' fifth inning spurt. Pitcher Hank Borowy sacrificed and Merullo scored when Gustine threw Stan Hack's grounder low to first base.

Both Borowy and pitcher Fritz Ostermueller of the Pirates encountered occasional trouble during the first five innings, the former giving up five hits and Ostermueller four over that distance.

Borowy's uncertain twirling got him in trouble in the sixth when the Pirates swung in front, 3-2, scoring two runs on as many hits. Bill Salkeld walked to start it. Then Bob Elliott singled, and after a force out, Babe Dahlgren walked to fill the bases. Pinch hitter Frank Colman drilled an outfield fly as one run scored and the second came across on Ostermueller's infield single.

Then, in the seventh, the Cubs moved back into a tie, getting one run on an error, Borowy's infield hit and Lowrey's single.

In the Cubs' half of the ninth, Hack walked and then advanced to second on Hughes' single. Lowrey sacrificed, and Phil Cavarretta was intentionally walked to fill the bases. At that point, Ostermueller was replaced by Nick Strincevich. Andy Pafko flied to deep to Barrett in right field, scoring Hack from third. Hughes advanced to third on the play, but he and Cavarretta were stranded when Bill Nicholson lined to Barrett.

The 1945 pennant-winning Chicago Cubs included Bill Nicholson, Frank Secory, Andy Pafko, Peanuts Lowrey and Ed Sauer (left to right). Also on the squad was NL MVP Phil Cavarretta, who led the league in hitting with a .355 average. In the Cubs' last World Series appearance of the century, they dropped a heartbreaker to the Detroit Tigers, four games to three.

4 Thrusts Give Chicago Cards the Title

By Harry Sheer

No crown ever nestled as firmly or as appropriately as the National Football League crown nestles on the Chicago Cardinals today.

Twenty-two long, humiliating years they waited for Dec. 28, 1947.

When it came, Sunday at Comiskey Park, the legion of red-shirted battlers did what most everyone said they'd do way back last September.

They whipped their Eastern Division opponents . . . in this case, Philadelphia . . . 28-21, with the same explosive thrusts they used to destroy nine out of 12 foes during regular season play.

Four times the Cardinals struck Sunday . . . actually ONLY four times in 60 nerve-wracking minutes.

Twice, Chicago's 22-year-old Elmer Angsman ran like some kid being chased by a cop for touchdowns . . . 70 yards apiece.

Twice, the Big Red $100,000 beauty, Charlie Trippi, ran with the zeal of a man chasing $100,000 . . . for 44 yards from scrimmage for the Cards' opening touchdown, again 75 yards with a punt in the most spectacular run of the longest season in NFL history.

That was all the Cardinals needed . . . four plays, four touchdowns, a dead bunch of Eagles . . . a championship, their first since 1925.

But there was a note of irony to the victory, and there were more than a few among the small crowd of 30,759 who sat in on the game who knew it.

The man who built these Cardinals into the most explosive team in football, Charlie Bidwill, died eight months ago.

He never even saw his Trippis, his Angsmans, his Goldbergs, his Harders together in the traditional Cardinal Red.

Angsman, the kid from Mt. Carmel, who can't see his hand in front of his face without his contract lenses, is the man of the hour today.

He had been pulling the Cardinals out of slumps all season long. Sunday, he merely added a few final touches.

The Cards, on the whole, played sluggish, almost desperate football against the Eagles. Except for the three line smashes by Angsman and Trippi, they were helpless against the tricky Philadelphia defenses.

And Pitchin' Paul Christman had his worst day of the season . . . completing only 3 of 14 passes for 54 yards.

But it didn't make a bit of difference in the final analysis. Not even with the brilliant passing of Eagle Tommy Thompson, who set two championship game records by completing 27 out of 44 passes . . . for 297 yards.

When the Cards needed a touchdown . . . they got it.

When they had to stop the Eagles, they did . . . even the fabulous Steve Van Buren.

Against that, Angsman ran ten times for 159 yards to smash the title-game mark of 109 yards set by Bill Osmanski of the Bears in that famous 73-0 playoff against Washington in 1940.

Members of the 1947 world-champion Chicago Cardinals await their departure for a road game.

17,823 See Trotters Beat Mikan, 61-59

By Gene Graff

George Mikan's one-man-gang demonstration amazed 17,823 Stadium customers Thursday night, but the Harlem Globetrotters lengthened their victory chain to 103 straight with a thrilling 61-59 basketball verdict over Minneapolis' Lakers.

Mikan's 24 points exploded like a pin-pricked balloon when slender Ermer Robinson connected with a desperate pitch as time expired.

The spectacle was billed as a private duel between Mikan and tricky "Goose" Tatum, Harlem pivot-clown, but the former De Paul giant was so superior, Tatum looked like a novice at times.

Mikan so thoroughly disillusioned Tatum during the first quarter the Trotters finally switched defensive assignments so that burly Babe Pressley could tangle with big George. However, Tatum resumed his apparently futile chase in the second quarter and Minneapolis carried a cozy 32-23 advantage into the second half.

Mikan netted two field goals in the first quarter and added three more and a free throw in the second period. Tatum, after being handcuffed completely by Mikan for eight minutes, finally entered the scoring column on a "sleeper shot" after loafing on his defensive chores.

The Lakers' Jim Pollard, using his six-foot-six height to advantage when the Trotters concentrated on Mikan, contributed five baskets during the first half. His rebounding, too, aggravated the Harlem quintet.

Mikan pushed his way through, over and around Tatum for two more baskets in the third period, but the Trotters climbed to a 42-42 deadlock at the three-quarter mark. During the rally, Robinson counted three from the court, and Wilbur King and Mark Haynes each added five.

Although Mikan fired in three baskets and two free throws, the Trotters held a precarious lead when Tatum departed on fouls with 90 seconds to go. Then big George calmly converted a penalty shot to knot the count, but Robinson's shot from the side swished through as the gun boomed for the Trotters' triumph.

No clowning around here. This 1948 clash between the Harlem Globetrotters and George Mikan's Minneapolis Lakers was a hard-fought, 61-59 victory for the Trotters.

Northwestern Charges Back to Stun Cal in the Rose Bowl, 20 to 14

By Jack Clarke

skinny little kid, who was christened Ed Tunnicliff at the baptismal font in his hometown of Kewanee, Ill., achieved immortality in the great saga of Northwestern football here New Year's Day.

Tunnicliff, who looks like he might get hurt playing with fellows much larger than himself, lit out on a startling flight of 43 yards with less than three minutes remaining of the 35th Rose Bowl pageant to provide Northwestern with a 20-14 victory over California.

Until Tunnicliff made his dash to fame, all from a Northwestern standpoint seemed lost but honor. After a 7-7 tie in the first quarter, Northwestern had gained the advantage, 13-7, at the half. Suddenly the fickle fates of football, who have been unkind to the Pacific Coast Conference in recent years, seemed to be showering their blessings on the grateful Californians. Capitalizing on a fumble, the Golden Bears went ahead 14-13 in the third period and Big Nine partisans in the huge crowd of 93,000 had reconciled themselves to their league's first loss in three years of inter-conference rivalry.

Then, in the dusk of this chill, cloudy afternoon, the Wildcats, with a mere six minutes to accomplish their heart's desire, fought back with all the fury their nickname suggests.

Shortly before, the jubilant Californians had advanced to Northwestern's 7-yard line, where the young men from the prairies successfully halted them. A bit later Frank Brunk, punting for California, booted a high kick to Frank Aschenbrenner on the Northwestern 1.

Aschenbrenner, who in the first quarter had sped 73 yards for the longest run from scrimmage in Rose Bowl annals and the touchdown that gave the Wildcats an early margin, carried this punt back to his 12.

Aschenbrenner immediately pegged his only pass of the game, a throw to Dan Stonesifer who reached Northwestern's 30. Gasper Perricone, on a lateral from Don Burson, raced 14 yards in two sorties. Aschenbrenner and Tunnicliff brought the Wildcats to midfield. For having 12 men on the turf the Golden Bears suffered a five-yard penalty but Perricone was ambushed and grounded on California's 48.

He got back to the 45 in two plays and Aschenbrenner collected an additional pair. It was here that destiny beckoned to Tunnicliff and the 22-year-old junior, who weighs a meager 165 pounds and stands 5 feet 10 inches, responded valiantly.

On a direct pass from center he darted through a gap in the left side of the line, twisted away from a couple of Bears who obviously harbored unfriendly intentions and ran and ran, as though pursued by a guilty conscience. He was apprehended on the 2 but his impetus carried him to his destination.

Jim Farrar, who had been perspiring on the bench in the belief that his missing Northwestern's second conversion would cost his side the triumph, pranced into the arena and toed the 20th and final point.

Members of the Northwestern football team begin practice for the Rose Bowl. It would be 47 years before the Wildcats returned to Pasadena.

cKinley Morganfield, better known as Muddy Waters, added the strain of electric blues to the cultural soundtrack that accompanied Chicago life in the 1950s. Before long, Chuck Berry had scooted his way onto the charts as one of a score of stars promoted by Chicago's Chess Records.

The whole town, it seemed, was jumpin', from the opening of the first McDonald's to the founding of Playboy magazine. The sports scene offered its own share of the action. Cubs fans finally finding something to celebrate in the wondrous Ernie Banks, who capped the decade with his 1958 performance, knocking in 129 runs and hammering 47 homers, all good enough to bring him the league MVP honors.

Is it any wonder he wanted to play two?

No matter how good Banks was, the White Sox managed to upstage events over at

Wrigley by winning their first pennant in 40 years in 1959. It was their initial season under new owner Bill Veeck Jr., but the dream run came to an end against the Los Angeles Dodgers in the World Series.

The decade, though, was known for much more—the Illini beating Stanford 40-7 in the 1952 Rose Bowl; Sugar Ray Robinson knocking out Rocky Graziano to regain the middleweight title that same year in a bout in Chicago; Robinson returning to Chicago to reclaim the title for a record fifth time in 1958; and Soldier Field hosting the colorful Pan-American games in 1959.

Among the home-grown contributions to the big time was the emergence of a 6-foot-1, 190-pounder out of Fenwick High on Chicago's West Side, John Lattner. He mastered several trades for Notre Dame—running, catching and punting—enough to earn the Maxwell Award as college football's top player for 1952, his junior season. He also excelled as a defensive back, intercepting 13 passes during his three-year varsity career.

The Irish opened the 1952 season ranked as the No. 10 team in the polls and promptly tied Pennsylvania, the 12th-ranked team, 7-7. The next week Lattner led them to an upset of fifth-ranked Texas, 14-3, but they were upset in turn the following week by Pitt, 22-19. From there, they whipped ninth-ranked Purdue, North Carolina and Navy to stand 4-1-1 going into their November 8 game with fourth-ranked Oklahoma, led by Billy Vessels.

Lattner and the Irish surged ahead in the fourth period as Notre Dame ended Oklahoma's 13-game winning streak, 27-21. It was a great win, but top-ranked Michigan State doused Notre Dame's enthusiasm the next week, 21-3. Rebounding, the Irish whipped Iowa and upset second-ranked USC to close out a good year. Lattner's all-around performance was enough to earn his first of two consecutive Maxwell awards as the top player in college football.

The circumstances surrounding Lattner's senior season in 1953 were hardly ideal. Notre Dame coaching legend Frank Leahy was in the midst of his last campaign and suffering from exhaustion. Lattner answered with a mix of leadership and athletic feats that turned what could have been misery into something memorable. Lattner opened the schedule by leading his team to a road win over sixth-ranked Oklahoma, 28-21. After that, Pitt and Purdue were the victims. Then the Irish faced fourth-ranked Georgia Tech in Notre Dame

Stadium. The Wreck was sporting a 31-game unbeaten streak, but Lattner returned the opening kickoff 80 yards to charge the Irish to a 27-14 win.

The Irish later tied Iowa, 14-14, but they remained in the running for the national championship. The next week they demolished Southern Cal, 48-14, followed by a 40-14 destruction of SMU. With that, the Irish finished 9-0-1. Maryland, however, with a 10-1 record, was voted tops by both AP and UP.

Regardless, Lattner was again a consensus All-American and claimed the Heisman over Minnesota's Paul Giel. Hail, Chicago.

The incomparable Ernie Banks came
to Chicago ready to play two.

It's Robinson by TKO!

By Jack Clarke

Sugar Ray Robinson, the ambitious young Harlem capitalist, added the world's middleweight championship to his hoard of valuable possessions Wednesday night.

After two minutes, four seconds of the 13th round, with Jake LaMotta, the defending champion, reeling drunkenly around the Stadium ring, referee Frank Sikora called the whole thing off. It was, of course, a technical knockout for Robinson who, by winning, must forfeit his welterweight title.

While Robinson and his jubilant retinue stood in the center of the scaffold, posing for the picturemen, LaMotta roosted disconsolately on his stool. Blood streamed from lacerations on his flat, gloomy face and his features mirrored all the tragedy of a world suddenly gone to pieces.

A throwback to the stone age, LaMotta, in the early rounds, lurched steadily forward. Vainly he tried to land a punch that would have knocked his opponent into an advanced state of rigor mortis.

Robinson, who dislikes being pawed, discouraged these intentions with a piercing left that persistently stabbed Jake's countenance. At first it seemed that Robinson's punches lacked the stunning authority of LaMotta, but the tide turned decidedly in Sugar Ray's favor in the 10th.

Several times Robinson rapidly retreated, momentarily stunned as though caressed with a blackjack. In the end, though, it was a triumph of mind over matter, for the overgrown welterweight champion had too much finesse, too much guile and altogether too much intelligence for a plodding, courageous but rough-hewn adversary.

A thin trickle of blood oozed from LaMotta's nostrils midway through the opening round, the first sign of wear and tear on either man.

In the third round, Robinson tried a change of pace, varying his jabbing left with a right uppercut, which caused the champion's head to snap back as though on hinges.

Robinson got his nose bloodied in the fourth, and LaMotta clipped him with a left to the chops that somewhat chilled his ardor.

The apparently indestructible LaMotta, who had been getting a boxing lesson from Sugar Ray, suddenly raked Robinson with a series of lefts in the sixth. For a time it looked as though Robinson might set an indoor record for the 50-yard dash, running backward, but this fast footwork enabled him to escape serious damage.

While LaMotta continued to stalk him as remorselessly as an income tax collector, Robinson got his second wind in the ninth. He smashed Jake's face with a flurry of sharp lefts that caused LaMotta, and the crowd, to wince.

For the first time, LaMotta seemed weary and ill at ease in the 10th. Sugar Ray, as agile as a dancing master, continued to impale him on that devastating left.

As the 11th opened, LaMotta ambushed Robinson in a corner and pounded him viciously until Ray escaped. Robinson then brought the crowd up roaring by clouting Jake from one side of the ring to the other. LaMotta's eyes were like glass and his knees buckled but he refused to capsize.

Practically defenseless, LaMotta was just a human punching bag in the 12th and the hysterical customers wondered how long human flesh could bear such torture. A deep wound under Jake's left eye was matched soon by a gash on the other cheek.

Then came the 13th. Robinson flogged LaMotta without a return until the abdicating champion slumped and embraced Sugar Ray around the hips. Here the referee stepped between them and called off the slaughter.

Sugar Ray Robinson edged Jake LaMotta for the world's middleweight championship at Chicago Stadium. Boxing during a time when heavyweights dominated the sport, Robinson was hailed as "pound for pound" the greatest fighter of his time.

Rose Bowl Champs Leave Stanford, Coast Stunned

By Jack Clarke

At a late hour Tuesday startled citizens of this area were still calling the newspapers to learn if that was an earthquake which struck that afternoon.

And Stanford supporters were suffering mental anguish more acute that anything even a New Year's Day hangover can cause. Here they were, confident that by the time twilight settled over the Rose Bowl their representative would be acclaimed as the first Pacific Coast football team to defeat a Western Conference troupe since the two leagues signed their business agreement six years ago.

But when the timekeeper mercifully brought an end to hostilities, Illinois had inflicted upon Stanford the third worst defeat in the half-century history of the Tournament of Roses, a 40-7 walloping.

Despite the scoring differential, the issue was in doubt until the fourth quarter when, with the suddenness of a volcanic eruption, the Illini tallied 27 points.

Illinois was the first to score, advancing 76 yards in six plays for a touchdown. Pete Bachouros went the final six yards.

Stanford retaliated immediately, going 84 yards in 14 plays to tie the score. Harry Hugasian plunged over from a yard out. Then Gary Kerkorian converted to give Stanford a 7-6 advantage which the Coast delegates maintained until the third quarter.

During the entire first half, Stanford, discouraged by the roadblocks set up by Illinois' line, resorted to the airlanes. Kerkorian completed his first six passes, thanks to some acrobatic grabs by Bill McColl.

In the second half, however, Illinois' defense grew more vigilant and Stanford's passes began to boomerang.

Midway through the third episode, a holding penalty, after the Illini had capered to a first down on the Stanford 2, unquestionably prevented an Illinois score.

A bit later, Stanford was making threatening gestures when Stan Wallace intercepted a Kerkorian sling on Illinois' 34 and made tracks for home.

Straight down the western sideline he raced, crossing midfield with no one close enough to flag him down. Then Norm Manoogian hurried over and wrestled him to the ground on the Stanford 12 after a 54-yard run.

Bill Tate ran to the 10 and Johnny Karras contributed five. With Stanford's defense massed, quarterback Tommy O'Connell resorted to a bit of deception.

He sent Tate wide around Stanford's left flank and the junior fullback completed his mission without interruption. Sam Rebecca added the extra point with a placekick and Illinois was ahead for the second time, 13-7.

Then, with Karras, Tate and Bachouros burrowing through gaps in the Stanford line, the Big Ten titleholders marched to the Stanford 7. There Karras was off and running. He crossed the goal, stepping high, and Rebecca toed the point.

In due course the agile Wallace intercepted Bob Garrett's pass. On the seventh play thereafter, Tate plowed across from eight yards away, climaxing a 43-yard excursion.

Not satisfied with this, Illinois then covered 60 yards in three plays, most prominent of which was a 41-yard hike by Clarence "Bud" DeMoss, freshman speed demon. He arrived at the 7 and Don Stevens scored from there.

Less than a minute remained when Stanford's Dick Horn, back to punt, was engulfed by a wave of blue jerseys and his kick blocked. Illinois took over on the Stanford 3. After a three-yard loss, Don Engels tossed a touchdown pass to John "Rocky" Ryan. Rebecca added the final point.

Illini quarterback Tommy O'Connell led the Illini to a convincing Rose Bowl win over Stanford.

Lattner Scores "Grand Slam," Wins Heisman, Maxwell Awards

By James Mullen

Johnny Lattner, Notre Dame's All-America halfback, made a small, graying woman the happiest mother in the world Tuesday.

Lattner, a 190-pound senior from Chicago, was named as the winner of the 1953 Heisman Trophy, generally recognized as college football's greatest individual award. In addition he won the Maxwell Award as the country's outstanding football player for the second year in a row.

"God bless us," said Mrs. Mae Lattner, when informed by telephone of the double honors heaped upon her son.

Mrs. Lattner, who resides in a small apartment at 5008 W. Madison, said: "We were hoping he would win the Heisman, and now that he has I'm certainly proud of him. He won the Maxwell last year, you know.

"Honestly, I can hardly believe it," she continued. "John doesn't tell us a thing. He was supposed to appear on a television program last Sunday in New York along with other members of the All-America team, and we didn't know he wasn't going to be there until they announced it from the stage. I had to call Notre Dame and talk to him myself."

Lattner, who prepped at Fenwick High School in Oak Park, received 1,850 votes to edge out Minnesota's Paul Giel for the Heisman Trophy. Giel was given 1,794.

In South Bend, Lattner said being named for the awards was "sure a thrill."

However, he added, "I'm sorry the team missed getting the top ranking in the national poll. We were all doing our best Saturday against Southern California, shooting for it. I seem to be getting all the honors and the team missed the big one."

The trophy perpetuates the memory of John W. Heisman, who coached at eight colleges during a career of 37 years. Billy Vessels of Oklahoma won the award last year.

Bert Bell, commissioner of the National Football League made the announcement in Philadelphia that the Irish "bread and butter" ball carrier had won the Maxwell Award.

It is named after Franny Maxwell, former Swarthmore College star and football referee. Lattner's selection was made by the Maxwell Memorial Award Club of Philadelphia, of which Bell is president.

In every game the rangy Lattner has appeared this season he has come through with a key play when Notre Dame needed it and it's on that basis that he was picked, the Maxwell board said.

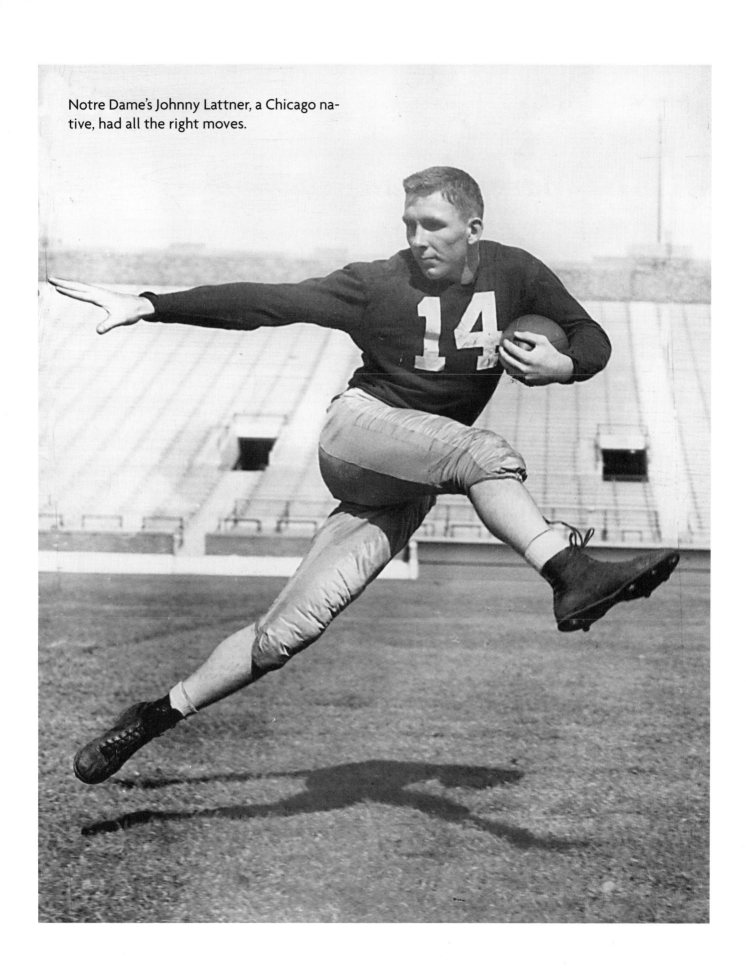

Notre Dame's Johnny Lattner, a Chicago native, had all the right moves.

Marshall State Champions

By Roger Yost

Chicago's Public High School League shed its scarlet letter of infamy Saturday.

Marshall's whirlwind Commandos defeated rugged Rock Falls 70-64 before 6,913 screaming persons at the University of Illinois' Huff Gymnasium to win the state championship.

The victory, Marshall's 30th in succession, gave Chicago its first state championship and distinguished the Commandos in another respect.

They became the fourth prep team to go through its schedule unbeaten in the 51-year history of the state meet. The others were Taylorville (45-0) in 1944, Mount Vernon (33-0) in 1950 and LaGrange (29-0) in 1953.

George Wilson, Marshall's 6-foot sophomore, picked up four fouls early in the game and was not as effective as he had been in earlier tourney games.

However, there was a young man named Steve Thomas present to take up the slack. Thomas, scoring baskets time after time in clutch moments, finished with 26 points.

Thomas, a lean, 6-foot 3-inch senior forward, kept the Commandos within reasonable distance of the Rock Falls squad when the latter began boring through the Marshall defense.

After a first quarter during which the teams swapped the lead frequently, Rock Falls emerged with a 20-17 lead. Still Marshall refused to topple.

The Rockets maintained the lead throughout the third quarter, after plunging to the front by 24-17 at its outset. A field goal and two free throws by Gary Kolb while Marshall was held scoreless hiked the Rock Falls lead.

But Thomas and 6-foot 5-inch M. C. Thompson, a bashful boy who is rough under the boards, combined to shave their debt to two points.

This was with 2:30 remaining in the first half. By this time, Wilson had acquired his third foul and was replaced temporarily by Paul Brown.

Jim Cain of Rock Falls also was guilty of frequent knavery and stepped out briefly after picking up his fourth personal.

Cain's substitute, Frank Simester, was even more effective. He pumped in seven points in a brief stint to put the Rockets ahead 38-32 as the half ended.

Thomas pegged in Marshall's final six points in the period, otherwise the Commandos would have been confronted with a Herculean task.

When the third quarter opened, Rock Falls connected with blitzkrieg precision, and the Commandos were down nine points, 43-34, a deficit they had never had to overcome at any other time this season.

From that time on, Marshall chiseled away at the Rock Falls stamina and lead—working an effective press and making two of every three shots.

Bobby Jones and Thompson joined Thomas in the stretch drive, through the last four minutes.

Marshall gained the lead 58-57 (the first time since it led 7-6 in the first quarter) on a 15-foot jump shot by Thomas.

Rock Falls retaliated with a field goal by Ken Siebel, regaining the lead. Then Bobby Jones tossed a line-drive jump shot through the hoop to give Marshall an advantage it never surrendered.

Wilson and Thomas scored four points apiece in the final three minutes to wrap up the victory.

M.C. Thompson (45), George Wilson and Steve Thomas (right) of Marshall High School take on Bernie Geers (41), Ronald Weigand and Bob Warnock (right) of De La Salle in 1958.

Sox Zero In!

By Jerry Holtzman

Pop the cork and pour those glasses full, the White Sox—that's right, Chicago's White Sox—won the American League pennant.

They won it here Tuesday night by beating the Cleveland Indians 4-2 before 54,293 at Municipal Stadium.

The victory, their 92nd of the season, gave the Sox their first championship since 1919, ending the longest pennant drought of any major league team. Now the Pittsburgh Pirates, who won last in 1927, have gone the longest without a flag.

It was the fifth pennant in White Sox history and the clinching was accomplished in dramatic fashion.

Gerry Staley, making his 65th relief appearance, came in and ended a ninth-inning Cleveland threat with one pitch.

The Indians had the bases loaded and only one out when Staley entered, coming on in relief for Bob Shaw. He threw one pitch and Vic Power grounded to shortstop Luis Aparicio.

Little Looie stepped on second and fired to Ted Kluszewski for the game-ending double play.

Staley was the last of three Chicago pitchers. Burly Early Wynn, who got the win, his 21st of the year, made the start.

Wynn was lifted with a 4-2 lead in the sixth. Shaw then came in from the bullpen and worked the next 2 2/3 innings until manager Al Lopez summoned Staley.

Al Smith, Jim Rivera and Billy Goodman led a nine-hit attack off four Cleveland pitchers. Goodman doubled across one of two Chicago runs in a two-run third and then Smitty and Rivera homered in succession off Jim "Mudcat" Grant in the sixth.

In the clubhouse after the game, manager Al Lopez went around slapping everyone's back and said, repeatedly: "Now, we've won the pennant. We've won the pennant."

Shouted trainer Ed Froelich: "What's the magic number now?"

"It's zero," someone yelled back. "A big, giant goose egg. It's zero."

"Isn't this a wonderful way to win?" asked Earl Torgeson. "We beat the team we had to beat. That's the best way."

Indeed, the Sox won by whipping the Indians, the only team with a mathematical chance for the pennant. The Indians are now 4 1/2 games behind, and even if they win their remaining four games and the Sox lose their last three, the Sox are winners by one game.

Staley, the team's star reliever, was mobbed in the clubhouse. Everyone was whacking him on the back.

A reporter elbowed through and asked: "What'd you throw Gerry? A sinker?"

"What else?" Staley replied. "I had to get him to hit the ball on the ground."

The 1959 White Sox won the American League pennant, the team's first since the ill-fated 1919 title. Only a Dodger powerhouse was able to end the Sox's great season, as Los Angeles bested the Sox four games to two in the World Series.

The Sporting News had declared in 1966 that Chicago was "long regarded as the burial ground of professional basketball."

Interred in the city's memory was a long list of failed teams with strange names. The Bruins, the Duffy Florals, the Studebakers, the American Gears, the Stags, the Packers, the Majors, the Zephyrs.

Although pro basketball had been around since the turn of the century, Chicago didn't get its first prominent pro team until 1925, when Bears maestro George Halas founded the Bruins to play in the American Basketball League. Both the Bruins and the league folded in early 1931, just as the Great Depression settled over much of the country.

Next came the Chicago Duffy Florals, who won the 1935 championship of the Midwest Basketball Conference, a forerunner of modern pro leagues. The Duffy Florals folded after a second season, and the city wouldn't feature another high-profile team until the American Gears began operations during World War II, a time when pro hoops showed a faint pulse.

Finally, the war ended, and in its aftermath came the formation of the Basketball Association of America. Chicago's entry was the Stags, set to compete for fans with the American Gears of the rival National League. The Gears and Stags both challenged for the championships in their respective leagues, but they still didn't draw much fan interest (although the Stags gave away an incredible 80,000 free tickets one season). Chicago just didn't respond. By 1950, all of the city's pro basketball teams were dead.

The city would feature no NBA team until the league granted expansion rights to the Chicago Packers for the 1961-62 season. The Packers got the first pick of the 1961 draft and took Walt Bellamy, the 6-11 center out of Indiana University who went on to win Rookie-of-the-Year honors by averaging 31.6 points and 19 rebounds. But the team finished 18-62 and found quick financial trouble.

The Packers changed their name to the Zephyrs, spent one more season in Chicago, then headed off to become the Baltimore Bullets. The experience seemed to finish Chicago as a pro basketball town. Dick Klein, though, found a way to raise money and to convince the NBA that Chicago could work. In 1966, Klein announced the birth of the Chicago Bulls. In reporting the move, *Sun-Times* columnist Dick Hackenburg declared, "Basketball is not dead in Chicago, it's just in a state of D. Klein."

For a coach, Klein chose Johnny "Red" Kerr, a South Side boy who had made good, first as a center at the University of Illinois, then during a long, distinguished run in the NBA. "I'm so enthused about it, I . . . I just itch," Kerr told reporters.

Jerry Colangelo, the Bulls' young marketing director, went to work trying to sell the city on pro hoops. "We had a parade," Klein recalled. "We got a great big longhorn from down at the stockyards and put it on a flatbed truck. The parade was two trucks; that's all we could get together. Even if we'd had every season-ticket holder in the parade, it wouldn't have been that impressive. We only had 176 season-ticket holders that first year. The press that came to the parade might have been giggling, but at least they were talking about us."

"We took the trucks down State Street, and the bigwigs were in a car behind us," remembered Ben Bentley, the team's first public relations director. "We sat in the trucks and we waved, and as we passed by, people said, 'Who's that?' They didn't know who the Bulls were. People were stopping and hollering at us. They were holding up their kids and showing them the bull and saying, 'They're gonna play basketball here. Basketball!'"

Johnny "Red" Kerr (center), the first coach of the Chicago Bulls, is the only coach ever to lead an expansion team to the NBA playoffs in its first year.

Hawks Stanley Cup Champions

By Jack R. Griffin

The injury-riddled Blackhawks, patched together with rookies, tried for the "big one" Sunday night that would give them the Stanley Cup.

Leading 3-2 in the series going into the game, the Hawks were trying for the victory over the Detroit Red Wings that would give them their first world's championship since 1938.

Missing from the lineup were Murray Balfour, who has a fractured forearm, and Dollard St. Laurent, who has a wrenched knee.

Two Buffalo farm club rookies, forward Wayne Hicks and defenseman Wayne Hillman, were brought in as replacements.

Coach Rudy Pilous kept his two rookies on the bench at the beginning, starting Al Arbour at St. Laurent's defense post and Ed Litzenberger at Balfour's right wing position.

Just past the midway point of the period, Jack Evans was chased for interference and the Wings began their harassment of Glen Hall.

Chicago managed to survive that two minutes but Evans hardly had returned to the ice when Arbour was whistled off for interference.

Hall was doing a big job holding off the Wings, twice stopping Bruce MacGregor at the goal mouth, but just before Arbour's penalty was up Howe started drifting deftly through the Hawk penalty killers.

He shot from about 30 feet and Parker MacDonald, standing near the net, tipped the puck toward the net.

Hall, in a semicrouch, seemed to have made the save, but the puck got away from him and dribbled slowly into the net under his bent knees to put Detroit ahead 1-0.

Two fantastic saves by Hall kept the Hawks unmarked as they went ahead with a pair of goals in the punishing second period, in which three players were injured.

With the Hawks outnumbered, Reg Fleming took personal charge of both defense and offense, finally scoring his first Stanley Cup goal at 6:45.

Fleming first stole the puck from Len Lunde, lost it to Pete Goegan, stole it back and swooped in alone on Hank Bassen for the score.

Right after that, Ron Murphy collided with Howie Glover, and the Detroit forward had to be helped off the ice and into the dressing room.

Late in the period, Ted Sloan was sent off for hooking and Hall had to make another cliffhanging save to keep the net clean.

This time Howe shot from the outside. The puck hit Hall's chest, bounded to the net bar, caromed up and was headed for a score when Hall finally grabbed it with his mitt.

As Sloan came off the penalty bench, he was fed a pass by Fleming and went in alone on Bassen. His short shot hit Bassen in the face and ricocheted away. Play was held up while Bassen got his eyes back in focus.

With less than two minutes left in the period, Bobby Hull made one of his headlong charges for the net. Bassen stopped him but was swept out of the net with Hull.

The puck, however, was left behind. Ab McDonald stepped up and knocked the puck into the open net.

That was the cue for Howie Young to bash Stan Mikita on the head sending him to the ice. Despite the flagrant blow, Ed Powers refused to call a penalty.

The third period had hardly started when Eric Nesterenko and Sloan had the Hawks ahead 3-1.

Sloan, carrying the puck, and Nester, following on the side, broke in with only one defenseman in front of Bassen.

Just before getting to the net, Sloan passed to Nester who lofted the puck into the net.

Six minutes later, Evans pushed it up to 4-1 with his first goal of the series. He bulled right through a swarm of Wings, kept the puck and went in alone on Bassen.

Goalie Glenn Hall and teammates Ken Wharram (17) and Dollard St. Laurent and the rest of the Hawks ruled the hockey world in 1961. When the victorious Hawks returned home to Chicago, they were feted by Mayor Richard J. Daley, who honored the team with the city's "Certificate of Merit."

Loyola Takes U.S. Crown 60-58

By Jack Clarke

Cincinnati's bold attempt to corner the college basketball market was hurled back Saturday and now Loyola is the power and the glory.

Thanks to Vic Rome's successful tip-in with one second of the overtime left the Ramblers wrested control of the national championship by overthrowing Cincinnati 60-58 in the National Collegiate Athletic Association final. In the process they ended the Bearcats' dream of becoming the first school in history to win the title three successive years.

In reverse this was the fable of the hare and the tortoise reenacted in living tableau. Cautious Cincinnati, using a wall-to-wall defense, attempted vainly to short circuit Loyola's high-voltage attack, but on this occasion, at least, the race was indeed to the swift.

Loyola was 15 points behind with 14 minutes left, but this team never knew the meaning of the word quit.

Defense has been refined to the status of an art at Cincinnati, and every little movement has a meaning all its own, but the Ohio River, now at flood tide, never broke through more dams than did Loyola.

In the final five minutes of regulation time and the additional five minutes of the added session, the Ramblers wove their offensive patterns while hurrying at full speed.

They shot from the hip, from the shoulder and while standing on their heads, and Cincinnati, accustomed to a more conservative mode of life, could not quite cope with this radically different philosophy.

In a way, Cincinnati's veterans resembled constables attempting unsuccessfully to throw up a roadblock against drag racers determined to burn up the town.

Cincinnati's defense throughout the season was the country's strongest, and Loyola's offense ranked No. 1.

Scholars will long debate whether Saturday's confrontation proved anything, in one way or another.

Except for a tie at 4-4, the first half was all Cincinnati, and the defending champions led 29-21 at the recess. Then after Cincinnati's margin had expanded to 15 points, widest of the night, Loyola began its magnificent comeback before 19,152 fans in Freedom Hall.

Jerry Harkness, highest scorer in Loyola history who didn't make his first point Saturday until 16:11 of regulation time remained, led the brisk counterattack. Finally with 4:18 remaining, he dropped in his first basket.

Moments later he stole a pass off Tony Yates near midcourt, dribbled in frantically and converted. His action set off a string of dramatic events. Loyola was then behind 48-43, but Ron Bonham added two points to Cincinnati's total.

Harkness followed with a free throw and a basket and Loyola closed in. Then Yates' free throw improved Cincinnati's position with 1:44 on the clock, but Cincinnati's George Wilson was accused of goaltending on Les Hunter's shot. Then Tom Thacker of Cincinnati and Hunter exchanged baskets, and Larry Shingleton looped one of two free throws, but just before the gun sounded, Harkness' vital shot plunged through, and an overtime was in order as the regulation game ended at 54-54.

In the extra period, Harkness' tap was matched by Wilson, and when Loyola's Ron Miller hit from far out, Shingleton balanced it at 58-58.

Loyola promptly controlled the ball, waiting patiently for the winning shot. It came, but not exactly the way it was planned.

Jerry Harkness, Les Hunter, Johnny Egan, Vic Rouse and Ron Miller (left to right) led Loyola to the 1963 NCAA championship.

Bears Capture Title 14-10!

By Bruce Morrison

Your Chicago Bears are still squeezing them out by the narrowest of margins, they're still leaning heavily on that heroic defense platoon, but THEY'RE THE CHAMPIONS OF THE NATIONAL FOOTBALL LEAGUE!

Before 45,801 of the fiercely faithful at Wrigley Field Sunday, the Bears rose up to smite down a favored New York Giants team 14-10, thereby winning the eighth championship in Bear history, the sixth since the league was divided into two sections in 1933, their first since 1946.

What was the winning prescription?

Maybe it was five interceptions that accrued to the darlings of the crowd, the Bear defense. Maybe it was linebacker Barry Morris, who was voted the outstanding player of the game. Maybe it was Bill Wade, who played valiantly and scored both the Bear touchdowns.

More probably it was a combination of many things, including a dedication to produce a victory for a founding father of the NFL who retains all the driving force of a 30-year-old. This was quite probably the happiest day in the life of George Halas who will be 69 on his next birthday. This championship was one the Old Man really wanted.

The New York offense had been said to consist only of the ability of 37-year-old Yelberton Abraham Tittle to throw the football. But Joe Morrison was the top runner of the day, with 61 yards in 18 carries, while Phil King added 39 in nine tries, and even ancient Hugh McElhenny (34) picked up 19 yards in seven carries and returned one kickoff 47 yards, getting past everybody except Roosevelt Taylor. Nobody got by Rosy

all day, but the little fellow took many a bump at his free safety position.

Tittle hit on three of eight first-half passes for 61 yards and one touchdown and had one intercepted. Then, at 6:35 of the second period, he was hurt, his left knee buckling as he was backing up to pass. Larry Morris was putting on the big rush at the time, but Y.A. thought he had done the damage himself, slipping on the hard ground. He came back in the third quarter (it was his idea) and had eight completions out of 24 pitches. But he also was embarrassed by five interceptions and seemed to lack his earlier effectiveness.

Wade was less effective than usual (10 completions out of 28 throws for 138 yards) but it was nippy (11 above when the game started), and despite weeklong preparations, the field became slicker as the game progressed.

Going into the final 15 minutes with the score 14-10, it looked like one of those deals where the fans—and the Bears—would have to sweat it out.

But that is reckoning without the Bear defense. First Morrison fumbled and Richie Petitbon recovered on the Bear 49. This opened the way for Roger LeClerc to miss a second field goal, but when the Giants pressed again, reaching the Bear 36, Bennie McRae intercepted a Tittle pass in the end zone.

Finally, the Giants found the tools to reach the Bear 39 as time ran out. With 10 seconds remaining, Tittle flung high and far again, apparently hoping that Del Shofner, or somebody would run under the ball and catch it.

Somebody did, but it happened to be the gallant Petitbon. And so a championship was won.

Mike Ditka used his hard nose for a face mask when he helped lead the Bears to the 1963 NFL title.

O'Hara Runs Record 3:56.4 Mile
as 18,307 Home-Town Fans Roar

By Jack Clarke

The way he ran and looked he might have been mistaken for Ichabod Crane fleeing the Headless Horseman.

As pale and spare as a spook, Loyola's Tom O'Hara won the Bankers Mile, feature event of the Chicago Daily News Relays, at the Stadium Friday, flowing the distance in 3:56.4.

His hands flopping like a rag doll's and his pink hairdo bouncing rhythmically, O'Hara thus improved by two-tenths of a second his own former indoor record of 3:56.6 established in New York a few weeks ago. Proceeding on the theory that he travels fastest who travels alone, O'Hara forged ahead shortly after the second quarter began and was practically unescorted all the way to the tape.

He was credited with quarter post times of 58.1, 1:58.8, 2:59.8. This means he hurried the final 440 yards in 56.6, a tremendous feat.

Along the way O'Hara also broke the record for the 1,500 meters, reaching that objective in 3:41.8.

Thus the young man who is studying accounting at the North Side institution further established himself as America's greatest miler and a leading candidate for the Olympic team that will compete in Tokyo next October.

Actually it wasn't even a contest. O'Hara lapped two hapless rivals and finished 50 yards ahead of Jim Grelle in second. Ergas Leps was third and Jim Irons, who set the early pace until O'Hara decided that the time to take charge had arrived, pulled in fourth.

Even so, O'Hara was not entirely satisfied with his good deed for the night.

"I expected Grelle to do better," the spindly little redhead explained. "I thought he would pull me out more; if he had I feel I could have run at least a full second faster."

Naturally O'Hara's 3:56.4 also gave him a new Relays record. Only a year ago he won the Bankers Mile in 3:59.5.

Actually the most confused people as O'Hara ran to glory were not the 18,307 witnesses, an indoor record crowd, but the mile judges. So awed were they by the Loyola scholar's accomplishment that they neglected to notice that Bill Dotson had been lapped.

So their original placings were subject to challenge, and it took them almost half an hour after the race was over to determine the order of finish behind O'Hara and Grelle.

Bears Roll; Six Sayers TDs

By Bruce Morrison

The name of the game, it says here, is spelled G-A-L-E S-A-Y-E-R-S.

Most of the 46,278 fans at Wrigley Field Sunday had expected the Bears to triumph over the San Francisco 49ers. A few had even thought the margin might approximate the 64-20 margin that became the final score.

But who ever thought that the first-year back out of the University of Kansas ever would score six touchdowns, gain 113 yards running, 89 by catching two passes and 134 more returning five punts?

Gale's six touchdowns hiked his total for the year to 24, one over the old National Football League record.

The six touchdowns by Sayers tied the one-game record held by Ernie Nevers of the Chicago Cardinals, Nov. 29, 1929, and William "Dub" Jones of the Cleveland Browns, Nov. 25, 1951. Oddly enough, both Nevers and Jones had their big days against the Bears.

Sayers, among other things, broke the Bear scoring record with 126 points for one season. It was set in 1951 by Johnny Lujack at 109 points.

Teamwise, the Bears were recording comebacks too. The 64 points formed a club record for regular-season play. The previous high was a 58-27 victory over Baltimore in 1956. The Bears' all-time high of 73 points was registered against the Washington Redskins in the championship playoff of 1940.

Chronologically, the Sayers touchdown parade went like this.

First quarter—80-yard run with pass thrown from Rudy Hokich.

Second quarter—23-yard sweep to left.

Second quarter—Seven-yard run, after taking pitchout and going wide.

Third quarter—50-yard run on fourth-down play with less than yard to go.

Third quarter—One-yard dive over the right side.

Fourth quarter—85-yard punt return.

Another record broken by Sayers was receiving the game ball from his teammates. It was the first time in history one Bear player has received two game balls in one season. Earlier, he had received one after the Minnesota game.

The Bears now have won five games in a row and nine of their last 10, and have beaten the two teams that now head them in the Western Division standings

Failing to win the division championship (still one of those calf-kill-the-butcher things) the Bears could settle for second. But even if they don't make that you can be sure of one thing:

For 70-year-old George Halas this has been a helluva year.

The Bears' Gayle Sayers broke the NFL season touchdown record in 1965.

It's Goal No. 51 And Hullabaloo!

By James Crusinberry

He had done it, this thing that no other player in the history of major league hockey had ever accomplished.

Bobby Hull had struck for his 51st goal, and he was grinning like a kid who had just been given the key to the candy store.

"It was the crowd," he said. "The roar from the crowd—I never heard anything like it in my life. I don't think I ever will again."

Forgotten almost was that the Blackhawks, after three dreary games of whitewash, had ended their long drought, forgotten almost was that the Hawks had roared out in the third period to beat New York 4-2 Saturday at the Stadium.

This was the Golden Jet's night, and more than 16,000 nearly hysterical fans were witness to a sight that nobody else in hockey has ever seen.

That 51st goal came while the Hawks still were trying to climb off the floor in the third period and blew them into a full-scale hockey team again.

Chico Maki had ended the long famine of 228 minutes 55 seconds without a score when he hit for the first Hawk score in four games moments earlier.

Then Hull, working off the power play, stepped into one, and he got his record-breaker in a manner that has been his trademark since he started breaking up hockey nets in the league.

The Rangers had almost worked off the slashing call on Harry Howell. Only 34 seconds were left when Lou Angotti shoved a pass near center ice at Hull.

"I started up the center," Hull said. "Their defense and their wingers kept backing. I stopped about 10 feet inside the blue line, and I saw they were still backing up.

"I shoved the puck out a little in front of me to get a good shot. But the ice was a little sticky, and it didn't go as far as I wanted.

"But I went ahead and shot anyway. I didn't really get a good shot. It hit just inside the post."

Hull pulled the trigger from 50 feet. It was a low shot, coming with the screaming speed that only Hull gives a puck in motion, and Cesare Manago never saw it as it went past him at 5:33 of the period.

"I just stood there for a minute," Hull said. "I wasn't sure. I knew it had gone in, but I wasn't sure that it might have hit one of our guys first."

But the crowd knew. From that mass of boiling humanity came a scream that must have caused the Stadium feet to tremble.

"That roar from the crowd gave me the greatest thrill I've ever had," Hull said.

The crowd held up the game for nearly 10 minutes, littering the ice with bats and whatever else was handy and throwable.

Hull finally skated around the rink, shaking hands with fans leaning over the glass, and then took the record-breaking puck over to his wife Joanne, sitting in the east end of the stadium.

"I was never so thrilled in my life," Joanne said. "Oh, I'm glad it's over."

The 51 goals broke a mark that has been matched twice, once by Bobby himself, but never surpassed in 21 years.

Maurice Richard first set the 50 goal record in 1944-45. Bernie Geoffrion matched it in 1960-61, and Hull did the same in 1961-62.

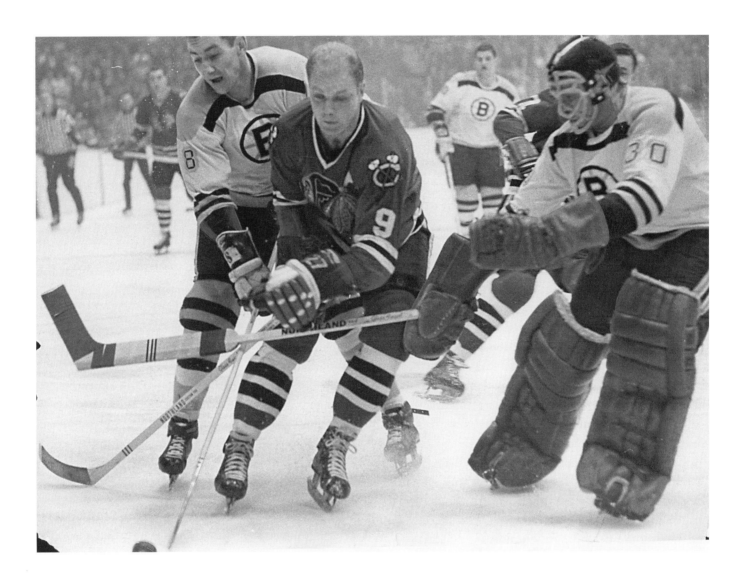

Named the NHL's player of the decade for the 1960s, Bobby Hull was a three-time point-scoring champion and two-time league MVP. Hull and his prototype curved stick made the slap shot a wicked scoring weapon and forced opposing teams to employ players whose only job was to shadow Hull on the ice. Hull retired from professional hockey in 1980 as one of the game's greatest all-time scorers, with a total of 913 goals (610 NHL; 303 WHL).

41,060 Watch Williams Break NL Ironman Record

By Jerome Holtzman

It was Billy Williams Day at Wrigley Field Sunday and, brother, did he take charge!

Sweet Billy did everything but carry the bass drum. In addition to tying and breaking the National League record for consecutive games played, he also knocked out five hits in leading the Cubs to a thrilling 3-1 and 12-1 doubleheader triumph over the St. Louis Cardinals.

The largest Wrigley Field crowd of the season, 41,060—a reported 10,000 others were turned away at the gate—paid tribute to Williams and saw the Cubs shatter their doubleheader jinx.

It was the first time in nine attempts this season that the Cubs won both ends of a twin bill, and for their efforts they increased their lead in the National League East to eight games over the second-place Mets and 14 over the defending champion Cardinals.

Williams had a day ball players dream about. He was honored during home-plate ceremonies between games and showered with gifts that included a new car and a puppy, and was also the big thumper in both Chicago victories.

His eighth-inning double helped break a scoreless tie and led to the first-game victory over superstar Bob Gibson. In the second game Williams really got hot and lashed out a single, a double and two triples.

The only thing missing was a Williams homer—the usual low-line shot into the right-field seats. A homer would have enabled him to hit for the cycle in the second game, but it made no difference.

The fans were so delighted with this opportunity to honor him that they even gave him a standing ovation when he struck out in his final time at bat.

The 31-year-old Williams never really has received his rightful share of the Cubs glory, not only this season but in other years as well. He has long been one of the National League's best hitters, both for power and average, and Sunday added his name on still another line in the record books.

He played in his 895th and 896th consecutive games, a remarkable seven-year endurance streak that began Sept. 21, 1963. The old league record of 895 was held by Hall of Famer Stan Musial of the Cardinals.

"I want to thank the Almighty God for giving me the ability to play major league baseball," Williams told the huge crowd as it hushed to hear his words during the special ceremonies. "I want to thank God for protecting me over all the games I've played."

This is the ninth full major league season for Williams, a native of Whistler, Ala., and he admitted in the clubhouse afterwards he was thrilled by the response of the Chicago fans.

"It was beautiful. It couldn't have been more beautiful."

Williams then revealed that he was somewhat nervous in anticipation of this day.

"I didn't know how I would react," he said. "I just didn't know what it would be like. I was here in 1964 when Ernie Banks had his day and I asked him about it and he told me, 'You're going to shed a tear.'"

Williams paused, as if allowing the day to sink indelibly into his memory.

"You know, I get paid for playing ball, paid well. It's something that you want to do and like to do. But this day was something extra. It shows me how the fans really appreciate me for the job I do in Chicago."

Billy Williams' ironman streak grew to 1,117 games before it finally ended on September 2, 1970. His record lasted for more than a decade before being surpassed by Steve Garvey in 1983.

Cubs Lose; Black Cat an Omen?

By Edgar Munzel

When the Mets were born back in 1962 as a bunch of misfits—discarded veterans and raw youngsters—they were so amusing in their stumbling, bumbling ways that their pixie manager, Casey Stengel, called them the "amazin' Mets."

But you can take the left-handed connotation out of that name now, because this 1969 edition of the New York Metropolitans is amazing for all the right reasons.

Paced by the hurling of their 24-year-old ace Tom Seaver, the Mets continued their mad pennant charge Tuesday night when they whipped the Cubs 7-1 for a sweep of the two-game series, before a standing-room-only crowd of 58,436 in Shea Stadium.

It was the fourth straight victory for the Mets and their fifth in the last six games, while it extended the losing streak of the fading Cubs to six, their longest of the season.

Thereby the Mets moved within a half game of the Cubs in the Eastern Division. And Wednesday the Cubs could now be knocked out of the division lead for the first time this season, since the Mets will be facing Montreal in a twilight-night doubleheader, while the Cubs are in Philadelphia for a single game.

And you can be sure that the frenzied new-breed Met fans will be out in force trying to root their heroes into first place. They were having a barrel of fun Tuesday night once the Mets had grabbed a commanding 6-1 lead in five innings.

Along about that time first one group and then another in the stands would burst into song to the tune of "Goodnight, Ladies" that went like this:

"Good-by Leo, Good-by Leo, Good-by Leo, we hate to see you go!"

In the first inning with Billy Williams at bat a black cat suddenly appeared on the field, scampered in front of the Cub dugout, crossed the infield between the plate and Seaver and finally fled underneath the stands beyond the Mets' dugout.

Whether it was just a stray or had been dropped onto the field by someone trying to put the hex on the Cubs never was established. But Seaver didn't need any aid from ancient superstitions.

The flame-throwing right-hander allowed only five hits and one walk and fanned five en route to his 21st victory, tops in the National League.

Seaver is only 3-2 over the Cubs this season, but in his last three starts against them he has allowed only two runs. July 9 he had a perfect game until Jimmy Qualls singled with one out in the ninth, and then he lost 1-0 July 14.

For a time it appeared that he might make another no-hit bid when he retired the first 10 men to face him. But Glenn Beckert doubled with one away in the fourth and tallied on one of two singles by Ron Santo.

It did little more than spare the Cubs the additional embarrassment of a shutout. They never really were in contention, because the Mets already had four runs by that time.

With the momentum the Mets now have, it will take a superlative pitching performance to stop them. On Aug. 14 they were third, 9 1/2 games behind the Cubs. Since then they've won 20 and lost only six.

But their domination over the Cubs started even earlier. After the Cubs had taken five of the first six games between them this season, the Mets now have won eight of the last 10 and have a 9-7 margin over the Chicagoans.

And what does Durocher have to say? Just two words—"No Comment!"

Was it the grind of playing in the daytime heat at Wrigley Field that wore down the '69 Cubs? Or was it just plain bad luck? Or was it the intervention of some supernatural force? The appearance of this black cat in front of the Cubs' dugout the day before the Mets overtook the Cubs would certainly argue in favor of the supernatural.

He came out of a Lithuanian neighborhood on Chicago's southeast side and made stops at Vocational High School and the University of Illinois on his way to the Bears and ultimate glory.

He is remembered for playing hard and playing angry. Dick Butkus knew he couldn't do one without the other, so he spent his time before games looking at the other team warming up, imagining that every smile was some put-down of him or his Bears. Years later, Michael Jordan would show a similar knack for turning imagined insults into motivation.

For Butkus, the aforementioned was accompanied by his own particular brand of bloodlust. "I wouldn't ever set out to hurt anybody deliberately unless it was, you know, important, like a league game or something," he confided during one of his first seasons in the league.

"I pray that I can get up after every time Butkus hits me," Packers running back MacArthur Lane said at the time.

Dick Butkus came to the Bears as a first-rounder in the 1965 draft, paired with another first-rounder, the gifted glider, Gayle Sayers. Bears Hall of Fame linebacker Bill George took one look at the sneering, 6-foot-3, 245 pound rookie and knew it was time to move out of the way.

"Football is something I was made for," Butkus said. "I gave the game all I could for as long as I could."

No one in or out of Chicago ever questioned that. In Bears annals, his competitive fury had few matches until the 1975 arrival of a young running back out of Jackson State.

Walter Payton quickly proved to be a redeemer for all those Bears teams of the 1970s. Remember them? Remember all the losses? All those cold, empty Sunday afternoons at Soldier Field?

Bears football in the 1970s wasn't so much a free fall as it was a sort of hopeless, miserable exercise.

Then came Payton. He rushed eight times in his first game and finished with zero yards. Observers said there were tears in his eyes when he walked off the field that day.

From there he proceeded to carve out a reputation for himself on the NFL's toughest proving ground—the muddy, icy, slippery fields of the NFC Central. For the most part, his was a bad-weather opera. Payton had a bum ankle that rookie year and sat out one game. From that point on, he played in 184 consecutive games. In 13 years, he missed only the one game.

It was in his third year of competition that he set the gemstone on which the rest of his career would be built: that dreamlike 1977 campaign when the Bears hitched onto Payton's determination and turned a 3-5 start into a 9-6 trip to the playoffs and league MVP honors for Payton.

For obvious reasons, the big day was Nov. 20, 1977, when Chicago offered its best bluster, cold winds whipping off the lake and gray clouds hanging thick with the threat of snow and freezing rain.

Payton had the flu. "During introductions, I was weak," he would recall later.

Payton ran 40 times that day for an NFL single-game record of 275 yards, and that prodigious productivity was just enough for the Bears to grunt out a 10-7 win over the Minnesota Vikings.

Series after series, he rolled out for that Bears sweep behind Revie Sorey. Time after time, he took on tacklers, shoulder lowered, knees kicking high. It was an image of relentless effort that he ingrained in the minds of his opponents, his fans, his teammates.

"I can give the man the smallest crack in the line and Walter will make two miles out of it," Bears guard Noah Jackson told reporters. "The smallest crack, a little piece of light."

Vikings coach Bud Grant watched Payton with admiration that day. "He was the whole package—runner, of course, but also a great blocker and pass receiver," Grant recalled. "Walter didn't play on very good teams, but he didn't miss a game, and he gave it everything he had to the last play, even if the Bears were losing by two or three touchdowns."

Like Butkus, Payton's performances left no questions—not in the minds of those who were there, who really knew, who saw him turn those little pieces of light into that burning fire.

Running emerged as a fitness phenomenon in the 1970s, with races becoming a popular weekend activity. Here, runners begin the Mayor Daley Marathon in 1978.

Ernie Hits 500th

By Edgar Munzel

Things could hardly have looked worse at noon Tuesday at Wrigley Field. The skies were dark and heavy with the threat of more rain, the field was soggy, and there seemed little chance the game would be played.

But, oh, what a beautiful day it turned out to be.

Ernie Banks hit his 500th homer and the Cubs climaxed the most glorious day of his long career by coming from behind to vanquish the Braves 4-3 in 11 innings.

And the two who eventually kept Ernie's big day from being marred by defeat were Billy Williams and Ron Santo, who with Banks have formed the Three Musketeers of the Wrigley offense for the past decade.

With the Cubs losing 3-2, Hoyt Wilhelm went to the mound for Atlanta in relief of a tired Pat Jarvis. The aged relief ace got a knuckler up too high, and Billy rocketed a 2-2 pitch over the right field bleachers into Sheffield Av.

It was Billy's 12th homer and sent the game into overtime. With first Ted Abernathy and finally Phil Regan holding off the Braves in relief of Ken Holtzman the Cubs came on to win off Bob Priddy.

Don Kessinger opened the 11th with a single to left. Glenn Beckert singled to center, and Williams was purposely passed to load the bases.

Santo then slashed a hit off Sonny Jackson's wrist with the Atlanta infield in and Kessinger trotted home.

"There was no way we were going to lose that game after Ernie had hit No. 500," grinned Williams. "But I was lucky I got a good pitch to hit."

Banks hit his historic homer in the second inning after Jarvis had a 1-1 count on him. It was a line shot that cleared the wall of the left-field bleachers by only a couple of feet, sailing in about 15 feet to the right of where the wall begins to curve.

The only thing regrettable about the entire afternoon was the small crowd, held to 5,264 by the rainy weather. However, the fans began screaming as soon as the ball came rifling off Ernie's bat and the roar was deafening when it went out.

Publicitor Chuck Shriver grabbed the P.A. mike and immediately announced that the fan who caught the ball would be given an autographed ball and a check for $250 if he returned it, because the ball was to be enshrined at the baseball museum in Cooperstown.

But nobody caught it. The ball apparently hit the concrete around the second row and spun back out again onto the field. Rice Carly grabbed it and tossed it to the Cub bullpen, and Willie Smith brought it into the dugout to Banks.

With that homer, his third of the season, Mr. Cub joined an exclusive company of only eight others who have reached the 500 homer plateau in the history of the game.

The others are Babe Ruth (714), Willie Mays (606), Hank Aaron (568), Mick Mantle (536), Jimmie Foxx (534) and Mel Ott (511).

"What a tremendous thrill," said Banks afterwards as he was interviewed on radio and television with the writers swarming around him.

"I want to thank all the fans and my father and mother, because they've all had a hand in it. I feel like the fans helped me to hit that homer last Saturday and again today."

Ernie Banks, holding the ball he hit for his 500th home run, salutes the crowd at Wrigley Field. Banks finished his Hall of Fame career with 512 home runs, which ties him for 13th on the all-time list of baseball's home run sluggers.

Thornridge Retains Crown

By Dave Manthey

Thornridge popped it all on the line Saturday night, the Falcons seeking their 54th straight basketball victory and second consecutive state championship in the Class AA finals against Quincy in Assembly Hall.

Thornridge waltzed to a 104-66 victory.

When Thornridge captured state last March in its first tourney appearance, the Illinois High School Association crowned only one king. Now there is also a Class A winner (Lawrenceville last week) as well as a Class AA champion.

Boyd Batts, who had his problems in the afternoon semifinals, was the complete player as Thornridge took the aura away from the championship by systematically working out a 57-26 bulge at halftime.

The 6-7 senior center scored 25 points, blocked shots, didn't get into foul trouble and even chased a loose ball off the court and returned it to an official.

It was a complete reversal, but it obviously came at the supreme moment when Thornridge needed an effort against a team that had blown apart the semifinals with some super shooting.

It was difficult to tell from the 31-point margin at halftime, but Quincy was in the game early at 14-12 on buckets by Larry Moore and Kelvin Gott.

Then Ernie Dunn converted a three-point play, and the Falcons were off winging. Quinn Buckner, who wasn't having a good tourney, was on the beam again along with Greg Rose, Dunn, Mike Boncyk, and, of course, Batts.

With Thornridge getting it all together like that in the first half (60 percent shooting and a 27-6 margin on the boards) there wasn't much Quincy could do.

The Blue Devils of coach Sherrill Hanks matched their first two periods of points (26) in the third quarter with another 26 and chipped five off the deficit, which was still sizable.

Thornridge toppled Peoria Manual 71-52 and Quincy whipped East Aurora 107-96 in a record-busting afternoon of semifinal action witnessed by the first full house of the meet—16,128.

It was an unbelievable exit for East Aurora, which shot 61.5 percent from the field. Only solace for coach Ernie Kivisto was that the 96 points set a record for a losing team and the Tomcats helped set a two-team scoring mark of 203.

Quincy's 107 also snapped the one-team scoring record in state play, bettering the 101 set by Rock Falls in 1958.

East actually outshot Quincy from the floor 40-37, but the winners were 33-for-45 from the free throw line as three Tomcats fouled out and two others were detected on four personals

Moore, although only 13-for-37 from the field, scored 32 points for Quincy. Reserve Gott contributed a super 25 and Sorenson had 20.

It was so tight that the score was tied 13 times, all by half time when the tally was 50-50.

In the opening semifinal, Thornridge was anything but a pack of super shooters. Buckner was far off and so was Batts. And Bonczyk was tired with a cold.

But Thornridge prevailed despite these problems thanks to excellent play by Rose and Dunn as the Falcons ran their winning streak to 53.

Rose scored 20 points on 10-for-17 shooting and Dunn chipped in a nifty 16 to more than cover the gap left when Batts and Bonczyk were on the bench cooling their heels with fouls.

Quinn Buckner holds the state championship trophy during the Thornridge basketball team's homecoming after winning its second consecutive title.

No. 1 Alabama Nudged 24-23 by Notre Dame

By Bill Gleason

Notre Dame is No. 1 by one. The Fighting Irish defeated Alabama 24-23 Monday night in one of the wildest games seen in the Sugar Bowl or anywhere else.

A crowd of more than 80,000 was on hand. More than 50 million were expected to follow the first meeting of the two football giants on national television.

While its defense held Alabama without a first down and to zero net yards in the first quarter, Notre Dame took a 6-0 lead with a 64-yard touchdown drive in seven plays.

The Irish started on their own 36, following a 44-yard punt. They went to the air for the first time with Tom Clements passing to Pete Demmerle for gains of 19, 26 and 14 yards.

That put the ball on the Alabama 3-yard line and it took Notre Dame three plays to score. Wayne Bullock cracked to the 1, Clements kept for half a yard, and Bullock knifed over behind a block from left guard Frank Pomarico.

The extra-point attempt was unsuccessful because of a bad snap from center.

Alabama finally got its Wishbone offense cranked up in the second quarter, but Notre Dame still led 14-10 at halftime on a 93-yard kickoff return by freshman Al Hunter—the longest in the 40-year history of the Sugar Bowl.

Alabama began by marching from its 20 to the Notre Dame 17 but defensive end Jim Stock forced a fumble by Alabama quarterback Gary Rutledge and recovered the bouncing football at his own 36.

Notre Dame's Bullock fumbled the ball right back to the Crimson Tide at the Alabama 48 four plays later.

The Crimson Tide covered the 52 yards in seven plays to take a 7-6 lead. The drive included a 15-yard pass from Rutledge to Mike Stock, no relation to the Notre Dame player, and an 11-yard keeper by Rutledge around left end.

Randy Billingsley cracked through the left side for the touchdown from six yards out behind blocks from Wilbur Jackson and John Rodgers. Bill Davis kicked the extra point, and Alabama led 7-6 with half the period gone.

The lead lasted 13 seconds. Hunter, a speed merchant from Greenville, N.C., took Greg Gantt's kickoff at the 7-yard line and zoomed untouched up the middle, breaking into the clear at his own 25. Clements passed to Denmerle for the two-point conversion.

Alabama narrowed the gap to 14-10 with 39 seconds left on a 39-yard field goal by Davis.

The lead changed hands twice more in the third period. Alabama, continuing to grind out chunks of yardage, stormed 93 yards in 11 plays following the second-half kickoff with Jackson belting up the middle for the final five yards. Davis' conversion gave Alabama a 17-14 lead.

Notre Dame took advantage of a big break when Richard Todd, Alabama's No. 2 quarterback, bobbled the ball while attempting to hand it off. Notre Dame's Drew Mahalic grabbed the ball in mid-air and lumbered seven yards to the Alabama 12. Eric Penick covered those 12 yards on one burst through the left side, making two nifty cuts en route to the end zone. Thomas kicked the point and Notre Dame led 21-17 entering the final period.

Bob Thomas, who had missed two earlier attempts, kicked a 19-yard field goal for the Irish with 4:26 remaining.

Ara Parseghian returned the glory to Notre Dame football.

Payton: Simply Brilliant

By Joe Lapointe

No dull game plan, no lack of offensive imagination can dim the brilliance of Walter Payton.

Sunday afternoon, football's best running back carried the ball on 40 of the Bears' 71 offensive plays. He moved it across the slippery AstroTurf of Soldier Field for a record 275 yards as the Bears beat the Minnesota Vikings 10-7.

Payton delighted 49,563 fans and astounded the television audience with a medley of sweeps, burrows, cutbacks and dives. He raised his league-leading rushing total to 1,404. His 275 yards broke the National Football League's single-game record of 273 set last Thanksgiving Day in Detroit by O.J. Simpson.

Payton, playing with the flu, raced through the Vikings like a virus, although they couldn't catch him. Minnesota, worried and wearied by injuries and age, was shredded by the 23-year-old, third-year running back from Jackson State who now has a chance at Simpson's record of 2,003 yards in a singe season.

"We swept right and left," Payton said. "I think we wore them down."

Payton scored the Bears' only touchdown and vaulted his team back into the pennant race in one of the NFL's weakest and most competitive divisions, the NFC Central.

Payton credited his success to God and his offensive line. "I didn't think I could put on a Walter Payton performance when I left the dressing room," he said. "I had hot and cold flashes. But I have faith in God. He will take care of you and he did."

Payton didn't seem impressed with his record.

"Maybe later it will mean something in three or four years or so, after I'm out of football," he said. "Right now, it's just another game."

He said he had no knowledge of the record until after he broke it with a four-yard carry around right end on his last run of the game.

"I don't like people to come up and tell me during the course of a game," he said. "It's something I don't like to hear."

Somebody asked Payton if there is any way he can be stopped.

"The night before a game," he said, "I would kidnap me."

Another great running back praised Payton and expressed concern for the Vikings. Chuck Foreman, who gained only 54 yards, said, "There's no limit to what Payton can do with that line in front of him."

BEARS NOTES: Walter Payton's best game until Sunday had been the 205-yard performance last month in Green Bay. That effort tied Gale Sayers' single-game Chicago record . . . Against the Vikings earlier this year, Payton gained 122 yards . . . he has passed 100 seven times this season . . . . He almost set another record for number of carries but fell one short of Franco Harris' mark of 41.

Walter Payton's single-game rushing record of 275 yards stood as the NFL's best rushing day for nearly 23 years.

Irish Crush Texas

By Randy Harvey

The masquerade is over. Notre Dame stripped the cover off unbeaten Texas Monday in the Cotton Bowl and discovered an imposter has been claiming college football's No. 1 ranking since mid-October.

No more. The Irish took care of that convincingly with a 38-10 victory that ended one debate and started another. Who's No. 1 now?

"This game puts us where Texas was," Notre Dame coach Dan Devine said. "I think we ought to be No. 1."

But Texas coach Fred Akers still hadn't realized after the game that the clock finally had struck midnight for the Longhorns, who were predicted to finish fifth in the Southwest Conference before winning 11 straight games.

"Sure, I still think we have a chance to be No. 1," he said in response to a question. "At least the team that beat us was a good one. Everybody can't say that."

That was a not-so-well veiled reference to Mississippi's early victory over Notre Dame, but the Irish didn't lose again in 12 games this season and became stronger as the season progressed. They peaked Monday.

"I don't think any team in the country could have beaten us," Devine said.

It was a particularly satisfying victory for Devine, 53, who has not been a popular coach during his three seasons at Notre Dame. He said last week he might make an announcement soon concerning his future and admitted after the game he had considered retiring.

"I decided in the second half I didn't want to do anything but coach," he said. "I decided I want to coach and as long as I coach I want it to be at Notre Dame. I wasn't going to quit if I lost."

By the time he made his decision, there was little chance of losing. The Irish had a 24-3 lead midway through the third quarter and led 31-10 at the end of the third quarter. They had a first down at the Texas 11 when the game ended.

"Where did we beat them?" Devine asked. "Just about every place that you can beat them."

But give the Longhorns credit. They helped.

"We had a bad day, man," said Akers, whose Longhorns lost for the first time since he became their head coach before this season. "You ever had a bad day? You saw ours."

So did a Cotton Bowl record crowd of 78,701 and a national television audience.

The Longhorns lost three fumbles and three interceptions, which brought back bad memories for some of their fans of the 1971 Cotton Bowl when an unbeaten and top-ranked Texas team fumbled eight times in a 21-11 loss to Notre Dame.

The Irish took advantage. They turned five Texas turnovers into scores, driving 27, 35, 10 and 29 yards for touchdowns.

But Devine insisted the Irish didn't receive any "lucky breaks." They might have scored 38 points anyway. It just would have taken longer.

Notre Dame finished with 26 first downs and 399 yards total offense.

The Irish expected to move the ball against the Longhorns. They didn't expect the Longhorns wouldn't be able to move the ball against them.

Texas' Heisman Trophy winner Earl Campbell gained 116 yards but it took 29 carries. The Longhorns abandoned their usual outside attack and tried to run through the Irish middle. It didn't work as junior middle guard Bob Golic had 17 tackles. He was named the game's most valuable defensive player.

When Notre Dame opened its 1977 football season, eventual star Joe Montana started the season as the team's third-string quarterback, having missed the entire 1976 season with a shoulder injury. By season's end, however, Montana was the starter and was beginning his championship legend by leading the Irish to the 1977 collegiate title.

De Paul Work Only Starting

By Ron Rapoport

The telegram from the governor was on the table in front of him. The phone calls from Chicago and Boston had subsided. His team, which was so tired that it had taken a nap before dinner, was tucked safely in bed for the second time that evening. The party in the room around the corner was rapidly doing away with a significant portion of the stock of the town's only liquor store.

It was Ray Meyer's night of nights, the biggest moment of his 37 years coaching, a night for total enjoyment and abandon.

But as much as he gave himself to it, accepted the congratulations and shared the delight of the De Paul rooters, there was a part of him that held back, that worried and schemed and hoped.

It was not Indiana State that occupied him into the earliest hours of Sunday morning. There will be time for that later. On that score he has what he wants: a berth in the Final Four, a 95-91 upset over UCLA that was as much a tribute to his coaching ability as to his team's talent.

"I'm going to sit at that head table in Salt Lake City," he said, thinking ahead to the NCAA coaches convention banquet, relishing how they had planned to honor him briefly as some relic from the past recently inducted into the basketball Hall of Fame, but how it would be different now. "I have my speech all ready: 'It took me 37 years to get here. Some of you young guys just be patient and wait.'"

This is the one he dreamed of and anything else will be glitter. "I never thought we would get it this year," he said. "I thought with good recruiting maybe next year." De Paul upset three good teams to get this far and captured the hearts and minds of the neutral customers it played before while doing it. With the Blue Demons' stylish gambling brilliance on the court and their easy, gracious warmth off it, they seem to have proved you can be a winner without arrogance or grimness or turning the game into an us-against-the-world crusade.

So you honestly believe Ray Meyer when he says he doesn't care what happens now. You honestly believe there will be no tears and no regrets if it all ends next Saturday. This is the week that is and they can't take that away from him.

Editor's Note: As every Chicagoan knows, De Paul dropped that Final Four game to Larry Bird's Indiana State team, 76-74. They rebounded in the third-place game, defeating Penn 96-93 to cap off one of Coach Meyer's greatest seasons. De Paul star Mark Aguirre played two more seasons before leaving as the NBA's top draft pick in 1981. When Ray Meyer stepped down at De Paul after the 1984 season, he was succeeded by his son Joey. Together, Ray and Joey Meyer coached the Blue Demons to 955 wins in 55 years.

De Paul coach Ray Meyer eyes star forward Mark Aguirre during the Blue Demons' run to the 1979 Final Four.

Butkus Moved by Fame Rites

Professional football greats Johnny Unitas, Dick Butkus, Ron Mix and Yale Lary were inducted Saturday into the Pro Football Hall of Fame in an emotion-packed ceremony on the steps of the domed shrine at Canton, Ohio.

Unitas and Butkus, both voted into the Hall of Fame in their first year of eligibility, drew the biggest response from the enthusiastic crowd of several thousand persons.

An emotion-choked Butkus said, "I dreamed of being a great pro football player as far back as I can remember. I consider being inducted into the Hall of Fame as the top of my dream."

Butkus, who retired in 1973, was the most devastating middle linebacker in pro football during his nine years with the Bears. Quarterback Unitas set many passing records in his 18-year National Football League career, the first 17 with the Baltimore Colts.

Pete Elliott, Butkus' coach at the University of Illinois and now executive director of the Hall of Fame, described him as "the yardstick for linebackers of all time."

"I wouldn't ever set out to hurt anybody deliberately unless it was, you know, important, like a league game or something."

—Dick Butkus

Selected as the Bears' top draft pick in 1964 (third overall), Dick Butkus excelled at middle linebacker in a way that still serves as the standard for all other NFL linebackers. He was named to the Pro Bowl eight straight seasons (1966-1973). He tops the Bears' record book with 25 fumble recoveries and he second on the Bears' list of total career takeaways (interceptions plus fumble recoveries) with 47. But his incredible determination and ferocity when he played the game stand far above any achievements that can be measured in a list. During his career, Butkus was the living embodiment of the Bears' "Monsters of the Midway" moniker.

You can have your choice when it comes to selecting the dance that dominated Chicago sports in the 1980s. Was it "The Super Bowl Shuffle" or the unpredictable ballet of Air Jordan?

Both, of course, put that extra-special gleam in the city's sparkle.

Before joining the Bulls in 1984, Jordan played on the U.S. Olympic team, coached by Indiana's Bobby Knight. Although Knight's systematic offense guaranteed him only limited playing time and scoring opportunities, Jordan's athletic performances during practices and games thrilled crowds and teammates alike as he led the United States to the gold medal in the Games in Los Angeles. "When Michael gets the ball on the break, only one thing's going to happen," said Olympic teammate Steve Alford. "Some kind of dunk."

"The excitement just sort of builds," agreed teammate Chris Mullin.

"Sometimes the players get into the habit of just watching Michael," Alford said, "because he's usually going to do something you don't want to miss."

After collecting his medal, Jordan repaired to Chicago to play for coach Kevin Loughery.

Former Bulls assistant Bill Blair offered this memory: "His second day of practice, Kevin said, 'Let's have a scrimmage and find out if Michael's as good as we think he is.' Michael took the ball off the rim at one end and went to the other end. From the top of the key, he soared in and dunked it, and Kevin says, 'We don't have to scrimmage anymore.'"

Jordan scored 27 in an early loss to the Celtics in the Stadium. "I've never seen one player turn a team around like that," Larry Bird, the league's reigning Most Valuable Player, said afterward. "All the Bulls have become better because of him. . . . Pretty soon this place will be packed every night. . . . They'll pay just to watch Jordan. He's the best. Even at this stage in his career, he's doing more than I ever did. I couldn't do what he does as a rookie. Heck, there was one drive tonight. He had the ball up in his right hand, then he took it down. Then he brought it back up. I got a hand on it, fouled him and he still scored. All the while, he's in the air.

"You have to play this game to know how difficult that is. You see that and say, 'Well, what the heck can you do?'

"I'd seen a little of him before and wasn't that impressed. I mean, I thought he'd be good, but not this good. Ain't nothing he can't do. That's good for this franchise, good for the league."

The Bears, the Super Bowl XX champions, were a curious mix of dastardly characters and sweetly silly stage hounds. The road show was led by William "Refrigerator" Perry, the monstrous defensive tackle and sometime-fullback out of Clemson whose size and gap-toothed grin made him a folk hero and a media-money machine spewing out endorsements with down-home ease. The ridiculous, sensational one was punk-rock quarterback Jim McMahon. His loud mouth irritated coach Mike Ditka, but he had an arm and a knack for winning. So he was tolerated. Then there was the incomparable yardage machine, Walter Payton, who had led the NFC in rushing five times since 1977. Other names cropped up with regularity—wide receiver Willie Gault, safety Gary Fencik.

Fortunately, the team had some very intense defenders. Otis Wilson, Mike Singletary and Wilber Marshall were the game's best linebackers. Richard Dent, Steve McMichael and Dan Hampton completed the defensive line.

Somehow the team clowns convinced its more respectable members to join a bit of video-age foolishness called "The Super Bowl Shuffle." The video, plus the blizzard of posters, books and other endorsements, all generated huge numbers—almost as huge as those the Bears generated on the field. They finished the season 15-1 (losing only to Dan Marino and the Miami Dolphins), then chilled the Giants, 21-0, and the Rams, 24-0, in the playoffs.

Finally, the Bears made a meal of the New England Patriots in the Super Bowl, turning the game into a 46-10 rout. Despite the runaway, that Super Bowl still drew 127 million TV viewers and millions of radio listeners.

Crews clean up the aftermath of the Bears' Super Bowl parade.

St. Joe's Stuns De Paul

By Mike Downey

his could have been one of the sweetest stories ever written. A story about a 67-year-old grandfather and his basketball team—a team that could have kept that great big smile on coach Ray Meyer's face for the rest of his life.

But De Paul was an accident waiting to happen. It was the top-ranked team in the country, the top-seeded team in the NCAA Midwest Regional and the top-heavy favorite to jump all over St. Joseph's of Pennsylvania on the way to Chicago's first major sports championship since 1963. This was going to be the season of a lifetime—Ray Meyer's lifetime.

It didn't take long for that season to crumble. Nine seconds. Nine seconds from the time St. Joseph's fouled De Paul's most accurate free throw shooter, Skip Dillard, the guy they call "Money" because when he shoots 'em they're as good as in the bank. Nine seconds from the time Dillard's miss was rebounded and rushed down the floor to an unguarded St. Joe's player named John Smith, whose lay-up won Saturday's game 49-48 and sent Ray Meyer's 39th Blue Demons team to the sidelines forever.

It was the only time the winners led in the second half. It was a game in which De Paul did not score a point—or take a shot—in the final 6 1/2 minutes. It was the lowest point total for the school since 1976. It was the lowest point total for Mark Aguirre (eight) since his freshman year. It was the lowest the players have felt since this happened to them in 1980 at the West Regional in Arizona.

That time, after being upset by UCLA, Aguirre hurried out of the arena and cried into the cactus. For a year thereafter, he was positive he would never have to hurt so badly again.

Saturday he did. After the shocking ending Aguirre tore off his jersey, threw it down (where a spectator claimed it as a souvenir) and stalked out of the building. He paced for a few minutes, then returned barechested to the locker room, where his teammates were crying.

Another Chicago play had closed on opening night. Another Blue Demon dream had died because another team like UCLA a year ago had played the game of its life. St. Joseph's was 24-7, but it was hopping up and down, full of life. De Paul was 27-2, all dressed up with no place to go. The players didn't know what to do.

Meyer did; he has done it before. He smiled. He said, "This is bitter, but life will go on." He said, "You can't commit suicide just because you lost a basketball game." He praised St. Joseph's strategy and stamina. He apologized to the people of Chicago for letting them down, but reminded them of the many exciting moments his team had provided.

By then, the locker room was empty of players. Meyer excused them with one piece of advice: "Don't let anybody see a tear in your eye." The coach himself wiped his eyes only when he saw Clyde Bradshaw, who had been to the NCAA Tournament for four years and had gone home empty handed.

Bradshaw walked aimlessly in the Dayton Arena parking lot, comforted by Vince Battaglia, De Paul's athletic director. He returned to the team bus, pausing only a minute to say, "It'll take a long time for the hurt to go away, but I can't let my life be ruined by this. There will be other days."

Dillard was the only other De Paul starter who was willing to face the press in defeat as he had in victory. He did it briefly, reluctantly, in a tunnel passage to the bus. "I can't really talk," he said. "I can't believe I missed it. The season's over. It was a good season, but it doesn't seem so important right now. That's all I can say right now, please."

Cubs Clinch!

By Joe Goddard

The Cubs scratched their 39-year itch last night.

In winning the National League East Division with a 4-1 victory over the Pirates, the Cubs hoisted their first flag since the league champion Cubs of the late Charlie Grimm in 1945, then drank to their memory.

"Back in '45, those guys were in the World Series. We know we have to win three more to get there, but I want our guys and our fans to enjoy this moment now. It's a moment for all of us," said general manager Dallas Green.

Today's manager, Jim Frey, hoisted his cap and tucked it into his jersey to thwart souvenir hunters as he rushed out to greet Rick Sutcliffe after a two-hitter that ended decades of frustration for faithful fans.

"You know, it's like sending your daughter to college," Frey said of a team that was 7-20 in spring training, including 11 losses in a row.

"One day, she's 18 and going away and she's still a little girl. Then, the next day, she comes home, she's a woman and she's gorgeous."

In becoming the major leagues' first 20-game winner this season and only the fourth in modern history to win that many for teams in different leagues, Sutcliffe struck out nine and walked none. "I didn't have good stuff at all," he said. "I must have thrown 50 change-ups."

The only hits were by .220-hitting Pirate rookie Joe Orsulak: a fourth-inning triple and a sixth-inning bunt single.

Sutcliffe, who will open the playoffs against the San Diego Padres at Wrigley Field next Tuesday, was so overpowering that only four outs were flies.

It was his 14th straight win, tying the club record set by Ed Reulbach in 1909. He's 20-6 for the season, having gone 4-5 at Cleveland before the seven-player June 13 trade that cost outfield prospects Mel Hall and Joe Carter.

Ryne Sandberg, whose pair of doubles led to half the runs, felt he was "going to burst" waiting for the last out.

Sutcliffe achieved it by sneaking a third strike past Orsulak. "I threw the heck out of that pitch," he said with a laugh.

When the Cubs finally threw their party, nobody came. Only 5,472 fans, more than half of whom cheered the Cubs, saw the historic game.

Almost half hurdled the rail to greet the players as they hurried into the locker room.

"Tonight is beautiful, it really is," Frey said. "We'll come back to earth in 24 hours. It will be a short-lived celebration, but we got to enjoy it tonight.

"It has been a long haul, seven and a half months since we all left home, uncertain of our future."

It was the Cubs' 93rd victory, the most since the last pennant squad went 98-56. The '69 team was 92-70 under Leo Durocher.

"This is just the start," said Keith Moreland, one of Green's first acquisitions.

"The playoffs are next, and believe me, those are the tough games. You play 162 all season, and it comes down to having to win three more.

"If we win those, the World Series will seem like a snap."

In 1984, Ryne Sandberg became the first Cub to be named the National League's MVP since Ernie Banks won back-to-back awards in 1958 and 1959. Joining Sandberg in earning league honors was Cubs pitcher Rick Sutcliffe, who captured the NL's 1984 Cy Young award with his record of 16-1 with the Cubs.

Records, Victory for Payton, Bears

By Kevin Lamb

The numbers Walter Payton liked best were 20-7, Bears.

Not that he was reducing his NFL rushing record to merely something that interrupted the Bears' victory yesterday, like a squirrel running loose on the field. The record meant a lot to him. After the season he'll send the Pro Football Hall of Fame his uniform in return for the ball he carried past Jim Brown's 12,312-yard pinnacle.

But if the Bears hadn't beaten New Orleans while he was breaking Brown's record, it surely would have taken the corners off his smile.

"You win, you can enjoy it," Payton said. "All these people in the locker room can celebrate, too."

The Bears' 4-2 record is their best after six games in Payton's 10 seasons. Their NFC Central lead is one game over Tampa Bay and at least two over the rest.

Even in the moments after he broke the record, Payton had the scoreboard on his mind. The Bears led by only 13-7 when he ran six yards around left end and five yards past Brown with 14:03 to play in the third quarter. The game stopped three minutes for the ceremonial backslapping and bulb flashing, fans cheering and eyes tearing.

"The thing I was thinking about was getting the people off the field, and maybe in the confusion we could get a quick score," Payton said.

The record hardly had been a shock. Payton went into the game 66 yards behind Brown, and as quarterback Jim McMahon said, "Walter's going to get 66 yards even if we don't block very well.

But Payton said it was an understatement to call him relieved. He had been in the national spotlight for three weeks, and although he took to it well, that is not his native environment. He would rather go fishing than be baited.

Now the media swarm will go away, at least until it returns for his assault on O.J. Simpson's single-season rushing record of 2,003 yards. Payton's 775 yards, a per-game average of 129.2, project to 2,067 for 16 games. He had 15 yesterday, breaking another of Brown's records with his 59th 100-yard game and moving within two of Simpson's and Earl Campbell's record of seven 100-yard games in a row.

"I can't believe how good he's looking," said Jim Osborne, the only other Bear besides Mike Hartenstine to have been active for all 137 games in Payton's career.

"He's running better this year than I've seen him run the last two or three years. The second effort's there. I saw signs of that slipping last year. He looks like the Walter of his younger years."

Walter Payton's NFL Achievements:

Hall of Fame induction: 1993
Super Bowl champion: 1986
Pro Bowl selection: 9 times
Career rushing leader: 16,726 yards
Career rushing attempts: 3,838
Combined net yards in a career: 21,803
Combined net attempts in a career: 4,368
Seasons with 1,000 or more rushing yards: 10
Consecutive seasons leading NFL in rushing attempts: 4
Most games with 100 or more yards in a career: 77
Bears' first-round draft pick: 1975
Set 28 Bears records during his career
Jersey No. 34 retired by Bears
Missed only one game in 13 seasons

Pete "Tys" It Up

By Ron Rapoport

With the cheers of another team's fans ringing in his ears, Pete Rose stepped across baseball's generation gap at Wrigley field yesterday and shook hands with Ty Cobb.

Rose ripped a sharp single to right-center field off Cub pitcher Reggie Patterson in the fifth inning to record the 4,191st hit of his career and tie Cobb for most hits in the history of baseball.

A crowd of 28,269 stood and cheered Rose as if he were one of their own, delaying the game for several minutes, as he stood somewhat uncomfortably at first base, waiting for the noise to subside and the game to resume.

"Don't move," Cub first baseman Leon Durham told Rose. "I want to get some TV exposure right now."

"With the count 3-2, I knew a fastball was coming," said Rose of the pitch he hit after Patterson had started with two strikes before going to a full count. "It was a fastball a little bit away that I got to right field." (Patterson said later both singles came off screwballs.)

Rose, who singled off Patterson's first pitch in the first inning and grounded out in the third, had two chances to break Cobb's record. But Larry Sorensen got him to ground out to shortstop in the seventh and after a rain delay of two hours and three minutes, Lee Smith struck him out on a 3-2 pitch in the ninth.

With the score tied at five, the game was called after nine innings because of darkness and will be replayed only if it figures in the race for the NL West title. All statistics—including Rose's hits—count in any case.

It was quite dark when Rose faced Smith in the ninth—though not long after the game was called the sun began shining brightly again—and when the hard throwing Cub right-hander took a little bit off his fastball, Rose swung through it.

"It makes it a little harder if you've gauged for a certain type of pitch," Rose said of his final out.

Rose wasn't supposed to play yesterday because Steve Trout had been scheduled to pitch and Rose doesn't start against left-handers. But Trout said he fell off a bicycle last night, injuring his left shoulder and elbow and Patterson was named to replace him several hours before the game.

"I didn't hesitate to put myself in," Rose said. "When I got the second hit, I looked at Trout in the dugout and he was pointing at himself, saying, 'Me! Me!'"

Rose has made no secret of the fact he wants to break Cobb's record in Cincinnati, which is his home town and the place he has spent most of his career. But he proved wrong all suggestions he was orchestrating his chase of Cobb so he could reach these milestones at Riverfront Stadium.

The hit that breaks Cobb's record could come as early as tonight in Cincinnati, although again Rose is not scheduled to play because the Padres are starting left-hander Dave Dravecky.

Asked what kind of hit he would like it to be, Rose said, "Just a line-drive base hit. Hopefully with a man on."

Superb!!! "46" Yields 46-10 Win

By Kevin Lamb

Champs again. Champs at last.

The Bears not only won the Super Bowl yesterday, they gurgled the New England's Patriots blood from it. Their 46-10 victory was the highest and most lopsided score in all 20 Super Bowls. The Bears decided the issue as suddenly as an all-out blitz and poured it on from there.

Just as they broke the Patriots like a fresh cracker, the Bears also broke the shackles of 22 years of futility and frustration. They broke both to smithereens.

They did it with dominating defense and opportunistic offense. They did it with the only percussion tune they prefer to "The Super Bowl Shuffle"—pads, popping, followed by spirits sagging.

"We played Bear football," quarterback Jim McMahon said. "I think they learned nobody intimidates the Chicago Bears."

They did it in their irrepressible manner of rowdy children, the kind teachers find both huggable and sluggable, and with the flair that has made all Chicago feel young.

"This is special," coach Mike Ditka said of the world championship cherry atop the Bears' 18-1 season. "We made history today. That's beautiful."

The Bears had more stars than an Airport movie. "No one key," Ditka said. "We played good football."

Richard Dent, the game's Most Valuable Player, set the tone with his two forced fumbles. He also had 1 1/2 sacks.

Jim McMahon ran for two touchdowns before leaving late in the third quarter. Wearing gloves, he passed for 246 yards, completing 12-of-20 without an interception.

Willie Gault caught four passes for 129 yards. His 43-yard gain was the second play after New England's field goal and set up Kevin Butler's game-tying kick. His 60-yard gain started a touchdown drive from the Bear 4.

Butler was 3-for-3 on field goals of 28, 24, and 24 yards.

Reggie Phillips had to replace Leslie Frazier at right cornerback when Frazier strained his knee. Phillips, a rookie, became the 24th Bear and 11th defensive player to score this season when his 28-yard interception return made it 37-3 with 6:16 left in the third quarter.

Rookie linebacker Jim Morrissey almost made it 25 and 12 when the scrubs were in for most of the fourth quarter. His 47-yard interception return was stopped at the Patriot 5.

William Perry kept the TV ratings from drifting during the rout. He played fullback at the goal line for the first time in eight games.

First, he tried to pass and became the first defensive lineman ever to be sacked in a Super Bowl. Next, he flattened linebacker Larry McGrew after McMahon faked a handoff to Perry and McMahon ran for a touchdown. Finally, he scored himself, from one yard out. He gave the Bears a Super Bowl-record fourth rushing touchdown and made the score 44-3 with 3:22 left in the third quarter.

Only a meaningless touchdown by the Patriots and another Butler field goal brought the final score to 46-10. And made the Bears champions again.

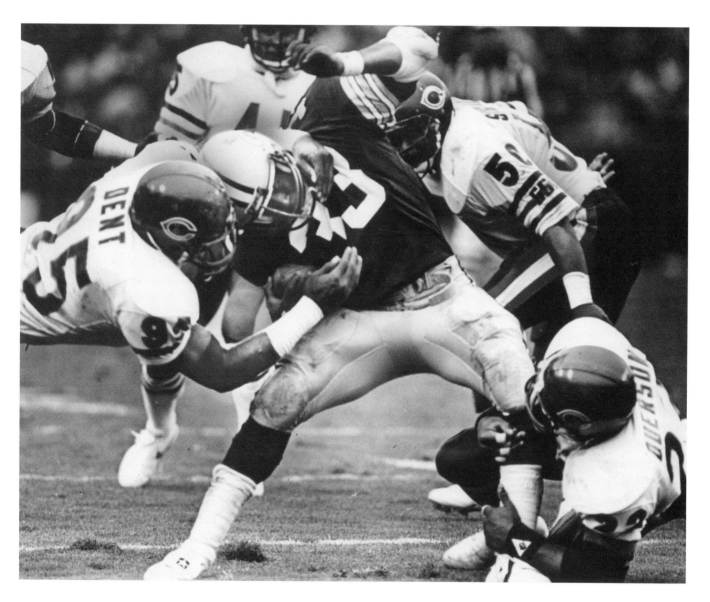

It was fitting that defensive lineman Richard Dent (95) was named the Super Bowl MVP. He led a dominating defensive attack that stunned the New England Patriots in Super Bowl XX and shut out the Bears' earlier playoff opponents, the Giants (21-0) and the Rams (24-0).

The Big Washout

By Joe Goddard

Light up, America! This game was for you.

It wasn't much of a gem. The Cubs were leading 3-1 after 3 1/2 innings of their first Wrigley Field night contest Monday when someone up there had a better idea.

It rained, and after a delay of two hours, 10 minutes, the game was postponed.

No contest. No score.

Fans can redeem their ticket stubs for later contests this season, but not for tonight's game. It's a sellout, too.

Rick Sutcliffe, who needed to pitch only one more inning to make the game official, knew exactly who threw a wet blanket on the sold-out picnic of 39,008 high rollers and low lifers.

"It looked the Good Lord said, 'I'm going to show you why Wrigley Field has always been in daylight,'" Sutcliffe said.

"He was pretty upset about this. He's telling us he'll determine when the first night game is."

The Cubs will try to play their first real night game tonight, but with a new opponent. Instead of the fifth-place Phillies, it's the first-place Mets, who are used to the kind of media attention that 556 members bestowed upon the old brickyard Monday.

Ryne Sandberg also had something to lose. He hit a two-run home run in the first inning and was the leg man in a third-inning run.

All records were wiped out by the unofficial contest.

"We had a chance to win; that's the most disappointing thing," Sandberg said.

"It felt good hitting the homer. The atmosphere was like an opening day or All-Star Game. The crowd was definitely buzzing. You could feel the excitement in the air."

Shining lights on their subjects for the first time in their 113-year history, the Cubs pulled the switch on a new era. They had been organized a few years before the light bulb was invented, but were the last team to install them.

"I thought it was a great night up until the rain," manager Don Zimmer said. "The lights were great. I asked their third-base coach, John Vukovich, if he thought the lighting was different here than anywhere else and he said no.

"I thought it was beautiful with all the white hats and everybody waving them. There are no better fans in the world than Cub fans."

Cub third baseman Vance Law said the lights were improved from the team's July 26 practice.

"You could see the whole ball instead of half the ball," he said.

Sutcliffe came to the park completely wrapped up in the occasion. "What motivates me is there is a lot of people and a lot of attention," he said. "Otherwise, I have mixed emotions.

"It's a great event. It's history. But to me, it's more sad than it is exciting. It's like two old friends saying goodbye to each other—sunshine and Wrigley Field."

Editor's Note: The first official Cubs game under the lights was completed on August 9, 1988. The Cubs knocked off the Mets, 6-4, for the historic victory.

Illini (Final Four) Real

By Brian Hanley

It was a day in which the colors of the rainbow to Illinois' pot of gold changed from orange and blue to black and blue.

It was a day in which the free throw line—Illinois' historic Bermuda Triangle—threatened to make championship hopes disappear.

But in the end, it also was a day in which this "small" team used the biggest muscle it possesses—heart—to beat one of the best teams in the country and send the Illini to the Final Four for the first time in 37 years.

The road to Seattle couldn't have been much steeper for the Illini (31-4)—a team that used two starters with bad legs to climb out of a 13-point hole Sunday and beat the 30-8 Syracuse Orangemen 89-86 before 33,496 in the NCAA Midwest Regional championship game.

Ironically, it was Kenny Battle, one of the Illini's walking wounded, who led the second-half charge with 17 of his game-high 28 points.

None were bigger than the two free throws he hit with 15 seconds left and Illinois clinging to an 87-86 lead.

The Illini hit only 3-of-12 from the line in the final three minutes—which assistant coach Jimmy Collins said threatened to turn this dream season into a recurring nightmare.

"I had flashbacks of Villanova," Collins said of the Illini's tournament loss last year when they gave up a 10-point lead by missing free throws on the front end of five one-and-ones.

"We definitely wanted to hold on to that lead," Collins said. "We certainly didn't want to have to go through that type of thing and the adversity that followed that game.

"I was just hoping that somebody over at the scorers table would speed the clock up."

But Battle, the man who took a licking, was happy he was the one who had the opportunity to keep the Illini ticking.

"At that time of the game, it's a kid's dream to have an opportunity to win a game like that," Battle said. "I just stepped up to the line and made them both."

He was also the one who stepped up the ladder first after the game to help cut down the net from the baskets.

Battle was soon followed by Kendall Gill (13 points), Lowell Hamilton (seven points, 18 minutes), Steve Bardo and Nick Anderson.

Since Anderson has been the Illini's human safety-net this season—catching the team every time it began to fall—it was only fitting he wore the twine around his neck after the game.

It was also fitting that Anderson, who had 24 points and a career-high 16 rebounds Sunday, was named the regional's Most Valuable Player.

He was joined on the regional all-tournament team by Battle and Gill.

The fact that they were joined on the court by Hamilton was almost as big a feat as the come-from-behind victory.

Hamilton, who suffered a sprained ankle during Friday night's game, did not start but played in a game his coaches thought he'd have to miss.

Hamilton, who was on crutches Saturday, insisted on playing, which Henson said is a trademark of his team.

"Desire, desire, desire. These guys wanted the ball," Henson said.

"They wanted this game. These guys are fighters. I've never had a ball club that fights harder than this.

"As I've said many times, they're not going to die, you're going you have to knock them out."

Steve Bardo (left) and Marcus Liberty crash the boards for the Flying Illini.

Shot Too Good Not to be True

By Terry Boers

he instant Michael Jordan put up The Shot Sunday, you just knew this time it was going to be true.

You knew it not because of the softness of his touch or the beauty of his follow-through or the trajectory of the ball as it floated toward the hoop. No, you knew it because there was not a chance that Michael Jordan was going to miss another game-winning shot.

While Jordan has long been playing basketball at such an incredibly advanced level that he can seemingly will things to happen, he did clang a jumper off the back iron that would have won Game 4 for the Bulls Friday night at the Stadium.

And Jordan, as is his wont, was tough on himself for that misfire. He was far tougher on himself, though, for the two free throws he missed in the final 48 seconds of that contest, which Cleveland won in overtime.

He was the guy, after all, who boldly had predicted it would take the Bulls just four games to dispose of the favored Cavaliers in this best-of-five playoff series, and the chance to do just that had slipped through his very own fingers.

That would seem enough to dissuade even Jordan from playing the role of soothsayer again, but with three seconds left on the Richfield Coliseum clock Sunday, he had one Tarot card left to play.

Tilting toward Craig Hodges on the bench during the final Chicago timeout, Jordan promised his downcast running mate he was going to make the winning basket.

The reason that Hodges was feeling rather poor had everything to do with the previous play. Assigned the task of guarding Cleveland's Craig Ehlo with six seconds remaining and the Bulls ahead 99-98, Hodges made one of the worst defensive mistakes you'll ever see.

After tossing the ball in, Ehlo, on a simple give-and-go play from Larry Nance, ran right past Hodges and scored the uncontested layup that gave the Cavs back the lead they'd held for most of the afternoon.

"I was jumping up and down trying to distract him [Ehlo]," Hodges said about his short nap. "He threw the ball in and blew by me like a streak at the same time.

"I was mad at myself, but Michael told me on the bench not to worry about it, that he was going to go ahead and make the winning basket.

"Michael just did what he always does—he really stroked it."

That stroke happened only after Brad Sellers made two snap—and correct—judgments. Sellers, the triggerman on the sideline inbound play, first took a brief look at Hodges, who'd squirted free.

Then he looked at Scottie Pippen, who also appeared to be in the clear.

But this was no time to play a hunch. Sellers knows no game is over until Michael Jordan says it's over, so he did the right thing—he gave the ball to him.

Although Ehlo stuck with Jordan so closely he actually made the Divine Mr. M. do a double-pump from the free-throw line, the shot rose unmolested.

The ball rattled on the rim for a brief moment, finally dropping in as the clock hit triple zero. Cleveland, one of the game's best young teams, was gone 101-100.

Jordan, as part of his celebration, turned to the sell-out crowd, which had been exceedingly rowdy, and screamed, "Go home!"—a move that he would later call "uncharacteristic."

"It's just that people were starting to talk to me about my tee times and how I'd choked," Jordan said. "I was also pumped up by the crowd here because they were trying to take me out of my game."

Of course, no one who ever has played the game can do that.

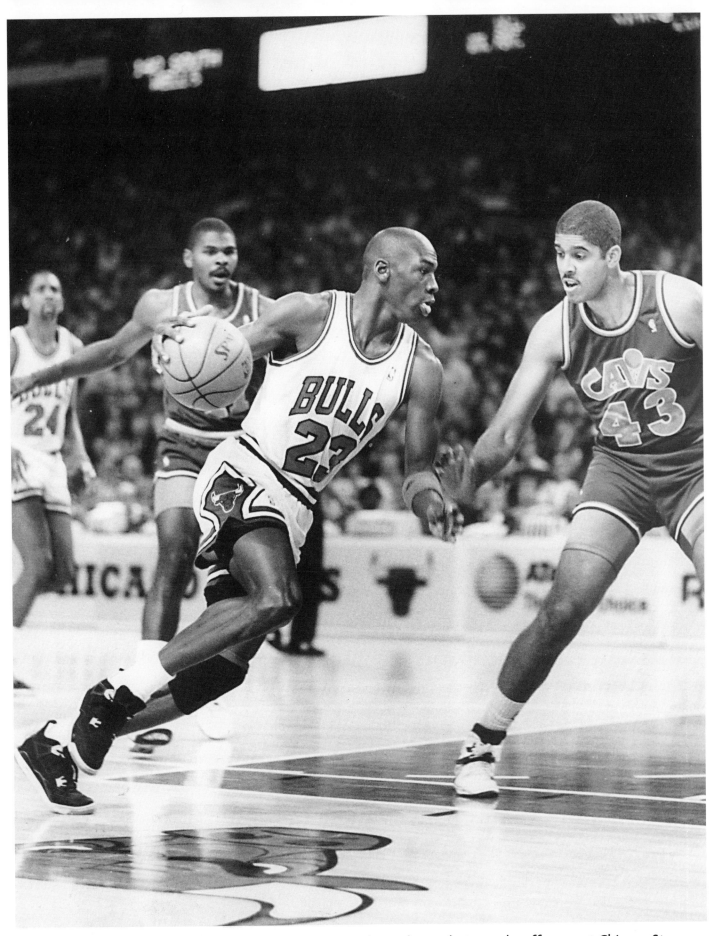

Michael Jordan drives past college teammate Brad Daugherty during a playoff game at Chicago Stadium. Four days later, Jordan would sink his famous shot over Craig Ehlo to send the Bulls to the second round of the playoffs.

CHICAGO'S
Greatest Sports Memories

1990s

Chicago's grandest decade opened with a demolition derby. Ancient Comiskey Park, a jewel when it opened in 1910, gave way to the wrecking ball and new Comiskey in the fall of 1990.

The nineties would come to rest sweetly in the minds of the city's sports fans, with Michael Jordan's Bulls claiming the first of their six National Basketball Association championships that June of 1991 and with Sammy Sosa's home run binge in 1998. But there were losses as well. The great Red Grange, "The Galloping Ghost" of Illini and Bear fame, died in Florida in January 1991. Two years later, in January of '93, the city watched the departure of a huge chunk of its competitive personality with the firing of Bears coach Mike Ditka. That July, just weeks after the Bulls claimed their third straight title, James Jordan was found murdered, prompting in part his son's early retirement from the Bulls in order to pursue a career in baseball with the White Sox.

The baseball strike stilled life for the Cubs and Sox in the 1994 season, and a loss to the Knicks in the playoffs ended the Bulls' dominance for a time. The slack was taken up by World Cup soccer as 1,800 journalists converged on the city to cover five games at Soldier Field.

The fortunes for the Bulls seemed set to turn ugly the following March, but Jordan's abrupt end to his baseball experiment and return to the hardwood brought back hope. While the playoffs that spring of '95 ended with a Bulls loss, better times were clearly ahead.

The karma was so good that the Northwestern Wildcats used it to boost their way out of the Big Ten's basement for a run to the Rose Bowl, their first appearance in 47 years. As big as that story was, it had a hard time matching the day-glo mania that the Worm visited on the Windy City when he appeared in Bulls training camp that fall. Dennis Rodman's strangely fun energy combined with Jordan's revived game to create an unparalleled display of power and swagger, the Bulls' record-breaking 72-10 season and delirious fourth championship.

On the fumes of that alone, the city could have zoomed all the way to the millennium. But there was much more—both good and bad—to be had, the Bulls taking their fifth NBA crown in '97 and their sixth in '98; Sosa's yard party the same year and the National League Rookie of the Year performance by the Cubs' Kerry Wood; the subsequent frustration of Woods' arm injury; and Jordan's final official announcement that he was done.

If only 1999 could have been skipped altogether, with its senseless, random, racist shooting of former Northwestern basketball coach Ricky Byrdsong, followed by the untimely passing of Walter Payton, which cut right to the heart.

Through their grief and anger, the city's fans were able to look back on a remarkable 10 years, the greatest 10 years of any city at any time, the testament for which had been provided courtesy of Jordan's farewell talk.

"I do know that no matter what happens, my heart, my soul will still be in the city of Chicago," he told the assembled media.

For the city so graced with his vast competitive spirit, that would be more than enough.

Six NBA Finals—Six Championship Trophies. The 1990s saw the Chicago Bulls build one of the greatest dynasties in all of sports history.

Back-to-Back

By Mike Mulligan

It's a moment that forever will live in Chicago sports lore—Michael Jordan and his fellow Bulls standing on the scoring table, holding up the NBA championship trophy to a packed Stadium crowd that wanted no part in leaving.

The Bulls became the fourth franchise in NBA history to win back-to-back titles with a 97-93 come-from-behind victory over the Portland Trail Blazers Sunday night. The postgame celebration in the old barn on Madison Avenue was as stunning and spontaneous as the unlikely fourth-quarter run in which the Bulls rallied from a 15-point deficit to oust the Blazers from the best-of-seven series, 4-2.

A year earlier Jordan sat in a locker room in Los Angeles and wept after winning that trophy for the first time. It was a personal moment of triumph, marking the end of seven years of frustration.

Things were different Sunday after the Bulls erased the largest deficit from which any team had rallied in the final quarter of an NBA Finals game.

Jordan, who had coddled the trophy like a newborn infant in Los Angeles, waved it freely at the crowd of 18,676 as the Stadium faithful danced along with the Bulls.

This one was for everyone.

"We went through a long test of adversity, me as an individual and our trials as a team," said Jordan, who became the first player in NBA history to win two consecutive regular-season and playoff MVP awards.

"It might not have all been pretty, but today we all stand tall."

Standing tall was a city that had not seen a professional sports franchise win a championship at home since the Bears in 1963, the year Jordan was born. Standing tall was a Bulls team that played through a season full of expectations and responded to every challenge it received. Standing tall were Scottie Pippen, whose play was continually criticized through the playoff run; Horace Grant, who fought off exhaustion; and Bill Cartwright and John Paxson, who played through both-

ersome knee injuries that might require off-season surgery.

Standing tall was a Bulls bench that responded when it was needed most with excellent fourth-quarter performances from Scott Williams, B.J. Armstrong, Stacey King and Bobby Hansen—no longer the only Bull without a ring.

"Last year it was a honeymoon," Bulls coach Phil Jackson said. "This year was an odyssey."

The Bulls trailed 25-19 after one quarter and 50-44 at halftime, and they trailed by 17 in the third period before taking a 79-64 deficit into the final quarter.

Jackson made a bold move when he decided to open the fourth period with starters Jordan, Paxson, Cartwright and Grant on the bench in favor of Hansen, Armstrong, King and Williams with Pippen, who was forced to take a leadership role.

The seldom-used Hansen got the Bulls going with a three-pointer and a steal.

King was sandwiched between Jerome Kersey and Kevin Duckworth while driving to the basket, and Kersey was whistled for a flagrant foul. King made one of two free throws. Pippen followed with a turnaround jumper off a post-up of Clyde Drexler.

Portland answered with a runner in the lane by Cliff Robinson, but King made two free throws, and Pippen added a bank, Armstrong a jumper and King another short bank to account for a 14-2 run that closed the score to 81-78 with 8:36 left.

"I was just a cheerleader on the bench," Jordan said. "I was afraid to come back in because those guys had such a great rhythm going. I was happy just to cheer for them because they always cheer for me."

"What a fourth quarter and what a way to win," said Paxson, who grabbed the rebound of Portland's final miss and dribbled in a circle before thrusting his hand in the air as the horn sounded.

"The fourth quarter was a clinic on offense and defense. Now everybody can go home for good."

"...17 down and they win it," was announcer Jim Durham's famous call of the Bulls' clinching victory in Game 6 of the 1992 NBA Finals against Portland. During the Bulls' rousing fourth-quarter rally, superstar Michael Jordan joined coach Phil Jackson on the sidelines as the Bulls' reserves whittled Portland's seemingly insurmountable lead from 17 points to a mere 3. Jordan took over from there and clinched the Bulls' second straight NBA championship with a 97-93 victory. But for many, the most vivid memory of the night will always be when the players returned to the court to join the Stadium crowd in singing and dancing to the victory anthem, "We are the Champions."

Triple the Pleasure

By Mike Mulligan

Perfect symmetry.

A game-winning three-pointer.

Three road victories

Three-peat.

John Paxson's three-pointer with 3.9 seconds left Sunday secured a 99-98 victory over the Phoenix Suns for the Bulls' third consecutive NBA title. The Bulls edged Phoenix 4-2 to become only the third team in league history to win three consecutive crowns. They join the Minnesota Lakers of 1952-54 and the Boston Celtics, who finished a run of eight in a row in 1966.

"Winning this championship is harder than anything I've done before in basketball," said Michael Jordan, who completed a three-peat of his own by being named the Finals MVP for the third consecutive year.

The finish was as dramatic as the Bulls' accomplishment.

The Bulls led by 11 points in the second quarter, led by 10 on three occasions in the third quarter and went into the final period with an 87-79 lead.

They then produced the lowest-scoring Finals fourth quarter—12 points, with all nine other than Paxson's three-pointer coming from Jordan.

For a while it seemed they never would score again as they failed to convert on nine shots and committed two turnovers before Jordan made one of two free throws with 5:51 left for an 88-86 lead.

That's more than half a quarter without a point.

Phoenix tied the game and led 98-94 with 2:23 left on two free throws by Kevin Johnson. In response, the Bulls committed their third 24-second violation of the quarter.

It seemed hopeless.

The Suns missed. Jordan missed with 1:29 left. The Suns missed two attempts to seal it, rebounded, called a timeout and missed a third.

Jordan grabbed the rebound and drove the length of the court for a layup to close to two points with 38.1 seconds left.

Phoenix wasted another opportunity to put the game away when Dan Majerle shot an airball on an open jumper from the right side.

Scottie Pippen grabbed the rebound and called a timeout with 14.4 seconds left.

"Do you guys want to go for it? Do you want to go for three?" coach Phil Jackson remembered asking in the huddle.

The Bulls came back on the court with a play that called for Jordan to drive. The Bulls star brought the ball upcourt and passed to Pippen at the top of the key. Pippen found Horace Grant cutting to the basket, and Grant whipped the ball out to Paxson for the open three-point attempt.

"It seemed like his shot took forever," Suns coach Paul Westphal said. "I knew we were all at the mercy of that ball and it's ironic that it all came down to everyone in the arena watching the ball come down and go through the basket."

Paxson—who underwent two knee operations since the Bulls' last title, including one during the season—calmly nailed the Bulls' tenth three-pointer, a Finals record.

"I got a clean look at it," he said. "There was no one around me. I just caught the ball and shot it as I have my whole life.

"When you're a kid shooting by yourself, you create games in your mind where you hit the shot to win a championship. It's been a frustrating year for me, but it just feels so good."

The Bulls had to make one more defensive stand. Grant, who scored only one point for the second game in a row, blocked a shot by Johnson to seal the victory.

"I'm not known for my offense so I had to do it with defense," Grant said with a big smile in the locker room.

Jackson said if Paxson's name wasn't a part of Chicago sports lore, it is now.

So are the Bulls. They boast a 13-5 Finals record in their three-year run—the best winning percentage in league history. They are also the best road team in the championship series with an 8-1 record.

The Bulls' starting five of (left to right) Bill Cartwright, Michael Jordan, Horace Grant, John Paxson and Scottie Pippen led the Bulls' 1991-1993 three-peat teams to a combined record of 185-61 (.752) in the three regular seasons and a combined record of 45-13 (.776) in the playoffs.

The Waiting is Over

By John Jackson

It was perhaps the shortest news release ever issued, but really, there was nothing else to say.

In two simple words, Michael Jordan said it all: "I'm back."

Back to basketball. Back to the NBA. Back to the Bulls.

"He walked in this morning, shook my hand and said, 'It's a done deal,'" Bulls coach Phil Jackson said Saturday after practice.

And just like that, what went from wishful thinking to a rumor to a possibility finally became reality.

"I hoped for it. I never thought it would be an actuality," Jackson said. "There's relief. We said earlier this week that this was a possibility, that this was coming to a head.

"For us and the fans, I think we're all relieved that this has been resolved."

Jordan will return today against the Indiana Pacers in a game that will be televised nationally by NBC.

"If this is what makes him happy, then I'm happy for him," Bulls owner Jerry Reinsdorf said. "I've always said I'll support whatever he wants to do. And he seems pretty excited about this."

Jordan has yet to address the media, but it's apparent that he missed the game and the competition more than he thought he would 17 months ago when he announced his stunning retirement.

In that announcement, which came days before the Bulls opened camp for the 1993-94 season, Jordan said he had little left to accomplish in the NBA and was happy his father had gotten to see him play his last game. Jordan's final game was in the 1993 NBA Finals and his father was slain two months later.

In December 1993, he launched a baseball career with the White Sox and spent last season with the Class AA Birmingham Barons. He hit .202 and was expected to be promoted to the Nashville Sounds in Class AAA this season.

But Jordan retired from baseball last week, saying its labor problems prevented him from making the progress he deemed necessary to become a major leaguer. Now he's come home to basketball.

Whether or not Jordan has made the right decision remains to be seen. But it's obvious his commitment to the Bulls is genuine and long-term.

"It's indefinite, as far as I know," Reinsdorf said. "I don't know how long he's going to play. He told me it's going to be for several years. But he can change his mind. I think that's something he has to address."

Jordan once again slipped out a back door of the Berto Center and in his burgundy Corvette zoomed by the mass of television crews and photographers gathered in the parking lot, leaving several questions unanswered.

How much will he play today?

"I don't know anything about what I'm going to do coaching-wise," Jackson said. "As of now, I can't tell you how long and when he'll play."

With just 17 games left in the regular season, can Jordan mesh with his new teammates—only Scottie Pippen, Will Perdue and B.J. Armstrong have played with him—in time for a playoff run?

No one was willing to tackle that one head-on Saturday. But perhaps the euphoria of Jackson and the Bulls players answered that.

"I think after having him on the floor tomorrow, I'll be able to describe it . . . maybe I won't be able to describe it," Jackson said.

"But once we see him out there in that red uniform playing for the Chicago Bulls, that'll be the emotional moment we've looked for and we've waited for."

Sunday Sun-Times

$1.25
Chicago/Suburbs
$1.50 Elsewhere

RAIN Pages 2, 63

MARCH 19, 1995

Late Sports Final

MICHAEL JORDAN HAD ONLY ONE THING TO SAY SATURDAY:

I'M BACK!

He'll Play Pacers in Indianapolis at 11 a.m. Today

Coverage In Sports

COMING MONDAY: A SPECIAL SECTION ON MICHAEL JORDAN'S FIRST GAME

Wildcats' Doubts Become Cheers

By Len Ziehm

Northwestern's formal Rose Bowl watch drew the same slow-arriving crowd Saturday that the Wildcats' home games at Dyche Stadium used to draw.

Sam Valenzisi, the injured placekicker, was the first player to arrive at Nicolet Auditorium—and the only one until minutes before Ohio State and Michigan kicked off in Ann Arbor, Mich., to decide the Big Ten's representative in the Rose Bowl.

"I might be the only one," Valenzisi said. "I thought about watching from my couch, but Coach (Gary Barnett) said there would be food. Anything for a free meal."

Attendance wasn't mandatory for the gathering, and only 17 players were there. Most of their teammates went home for Thanksgiving, though offensive linesmen Rob Johnson and Ryan Padgett headed for the Johnson family cottage in New Buffalo, Mich., and hoped to obtain tickets to see the game in person.

Offensive tackle Brian Kardos and tight end Shane Graham joined Valenzisi as ABC was completing its pre-game coverage.

"We're just waiting for (ESPN analyst) Lee Corso to pick Ohio State," Kardos said. "Then we know we're in."

Corso, who rarely predicted NU victories this season, never made a prediction on Ohio State-Michigan, but Valenzisi did.

"I think Ohio State will kill 'em," he said.

Valenzisi, the son of a high school football coach, grew up in suburban Cleveland but never attended an Ohio State-Michigan game—perhaps the premier rivalry in college football.

Three hours later, he knew all about how unpredictable that rivalry is. Michigan's 31-12 upset sent the Wildcats to their first Rose Bowl since 1949.

It was another glorious chapter in NU's improbable season, one in which the Wildcats ended a string of 23 losing campaigns with an undefeated Big Ten season and a ranking of at least No. 4 in the nation. With No. 2 Ohio State's loss, NU should climb even higher when the polls are released today.

"Now we could win the Rose Bowl, everybody else (No. 1 Nebraska and No. 3 Florida) could lose and we win the national championship," said linebacker Geoff Shein, a fifth-year senior. "Who knows? This is a magical year."

That was apparent throughout Saturday's game, played 250 miles away.

"We were right on the sidelines with them (Michigan)," Kardos said. "I don't think I've ever watched a game that closely. It was unreal."

"Watching it was harder than playing," wide receiver-punt returner Brian Musso said. "I'm more drained now than I would be after playing a game.

"We were nervous about this game all week, but it brought a great end to a fun year."

Editor's Note: Unfortunately, Northwestern's magical season ended just short of miraculous, with a 41-32 loss to Southern Cal in the Rose Bowl. In the game, quarterback Steve Schnur completed 23 of 29 passes for a career-high 336 yards and Darnell Autry rushed for 110 yards and three touchdowns on 32 carries. The Wildcats finished the season with a 10-2 record and a final ranking of 8th in the AP poll.

Gary Barnett's revival of the Northwestern football program to Rose Bowl heights was one of the most surprising sports stories of the 1990s. Before the Wildcats' 1995 season, it had been 47 years since Northwestern had been to a bowl game, and 59 years since they last won a conference championship.

Full Speed Ahead

By John Jackson

It was decidedly more difficult than the majority of the victories in this season of dominance and more of a struggle than just about anyone expected.

But in the end the Bulls' 86-80 comeback win over the Milwaukee Bucks on Tuesday night at the Bradley Center counted the same as all their other victories.

And with it, the Bulls became the first team to reach the magical plateau of 70 wins in an NBA regular season.

"Yes, I'm glad it's over. It's been a long time coming, 70 games," said Michael Jordan, who had 22 points but suffered through a 9-for-27 shooting night.

"I've said many times, we didn't start out the season looking to win 70 games. We set out to win a championship, and that's our focus now. It just so happened that we had some success early, some dominance very early, and here we are at 70 games.

"Quite naturally, it's going to take some time for this accomplishment to sink in."

Still, the Bulls did manage a mild on-court celebration moments after the final buzzer sounded—and in the locker room, cigars were exchanged like a gathering of new fathers.

"I must have had three cigars pressed on me at the end, victory cigars from the players," coach Phil Jackson said. "Although I'm not tremendously fond of cigars, I will probably smoke a cigar tonight in enjoyment of that."

The Bulls bested the 69-13 record of the 1971-1972 Los Angeles Lakers, and they have three remaining games to improve further on the mark.

In case the significance of the achievement was lost on the Bulls (70-9), the struggle against the Bucks (24-55) was a reminder of how difficult it is to amass that many wins.

"I think it let people know the games are still to be played," Jackson said. "For this basketball team, they've done a tremendous job at finding the clues to solve that puzzle that's presented to them every night."

The Bulls had hoped to put the game away early, but those plans didn't quite work out like they envisioned.

Milwaukee, coming off Sunday's upset of Orlando, came out like a team determined not to be upstaged on its home court despite having most of the sellout crowd of 18,633 rooting for the Bulls.

"I think this game is going to help us next year," said the Bucks' Vin Baker (game-high 28 points). "We were blessed to be in this situation. We were out there playing hard."

"We kind of put some pressure on ourselves," Jordan said. "Well, in the playoffs, there's going to be pressure every game. We didn't deal with it very well, and we'll have to improve on it."

Dennis Rodman, James Edwards, Michael Jordan, Toni Kukoc and Jack Haley (left to right) celebrate the Bulls' 70th victory.

Tiger's Town

By Len Ziehm

One lucky bounce. That's all Tiger Woods needed to join the impressive list of champions Sunday at the Motorola Western Open.

On the par-3 14th hole at Cog Hill's Dubsdread course, Woods knew where he stood when he took aim with a 9 iron, 107 yards from the hole.

Tied for the lead with Frank Nobilo, Woods decided it was time for a dramatic shot.

"I wanted to hit a high soft cut," he said, "and I overcut the shot. It was not a very good shot. It almost went into the bunker."

But it never got there.

Woods' ball hit a slope in front of the bunker and kicked to the right.

Woods grimaced.

"From a distance, it looked like it kicked pretty hard," Woods said. "I said, 'Oh, no!' I thought it might kick off the green, but it worked out. The golfing gods were definitely looking down on me in a good way."

And how. Woods' ball stopped a foot from the cup. He flashed an embarrassed grin.

With the raucous record crowd of 49,462 cheering him on, Woods tapped in for the birdie that gave him the lead for good. Nobilo's share of the top spot lasted all of three minutes.

"That was a knife in the back when he made 2," said Nobilo, who was playing two groups ahead of Woods. "But that's good golf for you. When Tiger gets

in position to win, he doesn't back up. We've seen it for the last 12 months—when Tiger needs to make birdies, he makes birdies."

The birdie put Woods in front by one. The 519-yard 15th—Dubsdread's last par 5—was easy pickings, as Woods hit a 4-iron from the left rough to just left of the green and used a 7-iron chip to five feet to set up his last birdie. Nobilo couldn't match him at the 16th, where his 15-footer for birdie missed.

That gave Woods a two-stroke lead. It reached three when Nobilo made bogey after a pulled 3-wood tee shot on the 18th. Woods finished three ahead with a 13-under-par 275 total for 72 holes to win the $2 million championship.

Woods really gave no one a chance. On Saturday, he devastated Dubsdread's four par-5s, making birdie on three of them to climb into a three-way tie for the 54-hole lead with Justin Leonard and Loren Roberts.

On Sunday, he showed his finesse, winning the title through stellar play in the four par-3s. He also made birdies on three of them, holing from 12 feet at No. 6 and 25 feet at No. 12.

"If I play my normal game, I should be able to win out here on tour," he said. "The biggest thing is to have the belief that you can win every tournament going in. A lot of guys don't have that. (Jack) Nicklaus had it . . . He felt he was going to beat everybody."

After crushing the Masters field by 12 strokes earlier in the year, Tiger Woods continued his mastery of the game by capturing the 1997 Motorola Western Open.

Kerry!

By Mike Kiley

There is not much reverence in baseball clubhouses. But Kerry Wood, a long-awaited gift from the baseball gods, had hard-bitten and grizzled Cubs veterans speaking in the hushed tones usually reserved for churches.

The tobacco-stained choir occasionally erupted in louder voices to sing his praises, trying to comprehend Wood's historic 20-strikeout performance against the Houston Astros at Wrigley Field, and as athletes do from childhood, fix a proper place for the accomplishment in their trophy case of memories.

After Wood's 2-0 victory Wednesday, the names of Sandy Koufax, Nolan Ryan and Roger Clemens, to name the usual Hall of Fame suspects, were evoked for yardstick purposes. At the age of 20, Wood is a long way from reaching Cooperstown, N. Y., but he seems to know the direction after just five major-league starts.

"I've played with three Cy Young winners," former Atlanta Braves infielder Jeff Blauser, now the Cubs' shortstop, said of the holy trinity of Greg Maddux, John Smoltz and Tom Glavine, "and I've been in two no-hitters, and this is as good a performance as I've seen. I'm glad he's on my team."

Cubs who didn't even play couldn't contain their excitement. They called out to reporters and each other to sit and share their thoughts. Everyone wanted to bear witness to an unforgettable event that should long withstand the test of time in a sport that again proved to be ageless.

On an afternoon that began under clouds and a severe threat of storms, the Texas Tornado from Irving, the home of the Dallas Cowboys, took the ball much like a running back and jammed it down the Astros' throats.

Wood's victory easily could have been a no-hitter if the official scorer had been stricter and figured third baseman Kevin Orie should have handled a ball to his left that skipped by his glove in the third when he decided not to dive. It was ruled a single for Ricky Gutierrez.

The only other baserunner against Wood was after Craig Biggio was hit by a pitch on the arm in the sixth. Other than that, Houston scrambled to come away with two fly outs, four ground outs, and a foul pop to first.

In the ninth inning, Wood fanned pinch hitter Billy Spiers on a 1-2 pitch leading off for his seventh straight strikeout. Biggio then grounded to shortstop on a 1-0 pitch. Wood tied the record by fanning Derek Bell on a 1-2 pitch and was mobbed by his teammates.

Wood struck out the side in the first, fifth, seventh, and eighth innings. He fanned two each in the second, fourth and ninth and one each in the third and sixth. He struck out the Astros' 3-4-5 hitters—Jeff Bagwell, Jack Howell, and Moises Alou—in all three of their at-bats, and he walked none.

Wood (3-2), who will turn 21 on June 16, set a National League record with his 20 strikeouts. He tied the major league record set by Clemens against Seattle on April 29, 1986, and matched by Clemens vs. Detroit on Sept. 28, 1996, for Boston.

Wood became the Cubs' strikeout record holder for a game. In 84 seasons, the most a Cubs pitcher ever struck out for a nine-inning game was 15. That was done by Dick Drott (1957), Burt Hooton (1971) and Rick Sutcliffe (1984). Jack Pfiester struck out 17 in a 15-inning game in 1906.

"I don't know what to say," Wood said when asked what this meant to him, to see teammates insisting they never had seen something like this. "They've got a job to do like I do. Today I did a good job."

Rookie sensation Kerry Wood was the architect of one of the most dominating pitching performances of all time: 9 innings, 1 hit, 0 runs and 20 strikeouts.

Three-peat Repeat Defines a Dynasty

By Elliott Harris

Forever.

That's how long this season has seemed to the Bulls. Or close to it.

"It's been a long and grueling season," Michael Jordan said.

Starting off with a trip to Paris for the McDonald's tournament, which helped super-size the season, and ending in familiar fashion.

A season that had Scottie Pippen missing the first 35 games because of foot surgery and Dennis Rodman behaving because of incentive clauses in his contract. A season of scoring supremacy from Jordan and soaring success from the Bulls.

Forever.

That's how long this season will be remembered. Or close to it.

As long as people discuss the greatest sports dynasties, the 1998 Bulls will be a part of the conversation. The repeat of the three-peat and sixth title in eight seasons puts the Bulls on the front row in the team photo of the greatest dynasties.

No question about it.

The only question is whether this is the end. It's a question that was asked and answered so many times in so many ways that no one knows. Not even today as the champions approach Grant Park for their annual rite of NBA passage.

"The Last Dance," coach Phil Jackson called the 1997-98 season in an effort to create a focus on the moment rather than the future.

Faced with not having the home edge in the Finals because the Jazz had beaten the Bulls in both regular-season meetings, the Bulls lost the series opener in Salt Lake City.

Maybe vice president of basketball operations Jerry

Krause and owner Jerry Reinsdorf were right. Maybe the Bulls should have been broken up to avoid an age-old problem of growing old ungracefully. Maybe the season had taken its toll on the legs and bodies of old hands such as Jordan (35) Rodman (37) and Ron Harper (34).

Maybe not.

The Bulls bounced back to steal Game 2 and bring the series back to the United Center tied 1-1. In Game 3, the Bulls took control, winning by a Finals-record 42 points and holding Utah to the lowest point total (54) in any NBA game since the introduction of the 24-second shot clock. A hard-fought 86-82 victory in Game 4 put the Bulls on the brink of another title.

But no home team has won the middle three games of the league's 2-3-2 format Finals, and the Bulls failed to clinch the crown in front of their fans, losing 83-81. So the Bulls won it the hard way in Game 6, overcoming Pippen's bad back and a hostile crowd to prevail 87-86 on Finals MVP Jordan's game-winning basket with 5.2 seconds remaining.

If it's the end, it finished with a flourish.

On March 27, an NBA-record crowd of 62,046 in Atlanta saw the Bulls beat the Hawks.

A little more than two months later, the Bulls had their second three-peat.

So now the question is Four ever?

Perhaps, if somehow Jordan is back and players and/ or coaches return or can be replaced to the point that leaves them a contender.

If not, there is always "The Last Dance."

One last chance to enjoy the moment. One more chance to savor the season.

A crowning accomplishment that will live on.

Forever.

HR Race Hits 66

By Mike Kiley

Sammy Sosa talked emotionally before the game of his foundation seeking to come to the aid of the injured and homeless in his native Dominican Republic, and then said the job before him was to lift the Cubs into the playoffs and take care of his business at home.

Sosa was only able to address half of that later equation. Despite his 66th home run Friday night, the Cubs lost 6-2 to Houston and failed to get a grasp on their wavering destiny.

A lost weekend against the playoff-bound Astros may eliminate the Cubs from the postseason. Their chances have become more complicated with San Francisco joining a three-way tie for the National League wild card with the Cubs and New York Mets.

The Giants beat Colorado while the Cubs and Mets lost. The New York defeat in Atlanta happened minutes after the Cubs left the field and drew a small cheer from the Chicago players as they watched on a clubhouse TV.

"What's upsetting is that we could easily have a two-game lead," said catcher Tyler Houston, who homered against the Astros.

Sosa at least commanded the attention of the world from which he is seeking donations when his 66th homer in the fourth knocked Mark McGwire to second in their race. This marked the second time Sosa passed McGwire, but his first rise to the throne expired after just two innings on Aug. 19—and so did this reign.

McGwire responded quickly to the challenge and ripped his 66th homer in St. Louis to keep Sosa from pulling away. The tie is a finish both players have said they would like.

"Mark said it would be beautiful to tie," Sosa said. "I feel great he hit his 66th. I had a good feeling about it. It would be nice if we tie. We just have to keep on going."

Sosa was playing McGwire and St. Louis on Aug. 19 at Wrigley Field when his 48th homer came in the fifth inning. McGwire hit his 48th in the eighth to tie Sosa, and his 49th in the 10th to grab back control of the competition most conceded he would win—including Sosa.

Sosa's 66th was Ruthian. He pulled a Jose Lima pitch into the third deck of the Astrodome in left field, an estimated 462 feet away.

The homer was Sosa's third off Lima this season. He took him deep twice Aug. 23 for his 50th and 51st homes.

Editor's Note: Sammy Sosa's 66 historic blasts in 1998 helped extend the Cubs' season by an extra game when they faced the San Francisco Giants to determine the final spot in the 1998 NL playoffs. The Cubs defeated the Giants 5-3 at Wrigley Field to advance to the Division Series against Atlanta. The Braves, however, swept the Cubs out of the playoffs.

While Sammy Sosa's home runs garnered most of the public's attention, it was Sosa's enthusiasm and goodwill for the game of baseball that made 1998 truly one of the greatest baseball seasons of all time.

Rout of Passage

By Jeanie Chung

The largest crowd to see a soccer game at Soldier Field, 65,080, cheered wildly at every U.S. touch on the ball, waved flags and chanted "USA! USA!" at every opportunity.

It was a crowd cheering for a victory, and for a lot of goals, and its team did not disappoint, beating Nigeria 7-1 Thursday in the first round of the Women's World Cup.

"If someone had said, 'The score's going to be 7-1 against Nigeria,' I would have said, 'No way,'" U.S. defender Brandi Chastain said. "They're a good team."

But the United States was better. Its seven goals were the most it has scored in a World Cup match since beating Chinese Taipei 7-0 in the quarterfinals in 1991.

Forward Tiffeny Milbrett scored two goals. Mia Hamm scored her 111th career goal and added an assist.

U.S. coach Tony DiCicco predicted the Nigerians would be a dangerous team, and the Super Falcons proved him right in the second minute, as midfielder Nkiru Okosieme gave Nigeria a 1-0 lead. Forward Mercy Akide sent a through ball to a charging Okosieme, who put it in the lower right corner. U.S. keeper Briana Scurry had no chance on the shot.

The United States prides itself on not giving up any goals, let alone one in the first two minutes. Therefore, none of the players said anything to each other after Okosieme's goal.

"I don't think we had to," U.S. midfielder Kristine Lilly said. "We all knew what was going to happen next."

As quickly as things had gone wrong for the United states, they turned around dramatically 15 minutes later. In the 19th minute, Hamm took a free kick from out-side the left side of the penalty area. It originally appeared that midfielder Michelle Akers poked the ball in with her right toe, but officials later ruled it an own goal off Nigerian defender Ifeanyichukwu Chiejene.

A minute later, Hamm scored on a buildup from the back that began with U.S. defender Kate Sobrero. Sobrero played a ball to Lilly, who found Hamm on the right side. Hamm evaded Nigerian defender Kikelomo Ajayi and put away her breakaway on goalkeeper Ann Chiejine to make it 2-1.

In the 23rd minute, Milbrett sent a cross from the right side to Lilly in the middle. Lilly's shot bounced off a defender, but Cindy Parlow collected the rebound and sent it back out to Milbrett, who knocked it in.

Big, fast and physical, the Super Falcons played smothering defense early on the U.S. attack, especially on Hamm. In the ninth minute, Ajayi took Hamm down from behind and, despite DiCicco's protests, was not shown a card. He called the physical play in the game "close to being out of control."

But once the dam broke, nothing Nigeria did could stop the United States.

"Putting the ball in the back of the net is the best way to slow down a team as strong physically as Nigeria," DiCicco said.

In the 32nd minute, Hamm took another free kick from the left side of the box, and Lilly headed it in to make it 4-1 and essentially put the game out of reach.

"She was talking to me at halftime, saying, 'I wasn't sure if you saw me,'" Hamm said of Lilly. "Kristine's legendary in the box. She does a wonderful job slashing in there."

Mia Hamm and her teammates practice at Illinois Benedictine University in Lisle, Illinois, before their opening-round game against Nigeria.

CHICAGO'S
Greatest Sports Memories